Assessment for Prevention and Early Intervention (K-3)

Second Edition

Louisa C. Moats, Ed.D.

Carrie Hancock, Ph.D.

and

Contributing Author J. Ron Nelson

Presenter's Kit by Carol Tolman, Ed.D.

Printed in the United States of America
Published and distributed by

17855 Dallas Parkway, Suite 400 • Dallas, TX 75287 • 800 547-6747
www.voyagersopris.com

How does copyright pertain to LETRS® Module 8?

- It is illegal to reproduce any part of the LETRS Module 8 book in any way and for any reason without written permission from the copyright holder, Cambium Learning® Sopris. This applies to copying, scanning, retyping, etc.
- It is illegal to reproduce LETRS Module 8 materials to distribute or present at a workshop without written permission from the copyright holder.
- It is illegal to use the name LETRS in association with any workshop, materials, training, publications, etc., without written permission from the copyright holder.

Acknowledgments

The LETRS modules have been developed with the help of many people. The National LETRS Trainers—who currently include Carol Tolman, Mary Dahlgren, Nancy Hennessy, Susan Hall, Deb Glaser, Judi Dodson, Pat Sekel, Anthony Fierro, and Anne Whitney—have all offered valuable suggestions for improving the module content and structure. Carol Tolman gave me feedback and invaluable assistance finding flaws in an earlier draft. Linda Farrell, formerly a LETRS trainer, generously contributed case study material and permission to publish Really Great Reading Company's diagnostic decoding survey. Pati Montgomery supplied case study data from schools she has lead or guided in Colorado. Bruce Rosow, Kevin Feldman, Susan Lowell, Patricia Mathes, Marianne Steverson, Lynn Kuhn, Jan Hasbrouck, Marsha Berger, Susan Smartt, and Nancy Eberhardt all contributed their expertise to the first edition of LETRS. Ron Nelson provided a crucial Appendix for the Early Childhood module that was adopted for this one. Many other professionals from all over the country who have attended institutes and offered constructive criticism have enabled the continual improvement of LETRS and related materials. I hope you see your influence on the revised editions.

I am grateful for the competent support of the Sopris editorial and production staff—past and present—including Stu Horsfall, Holly Bell, Jeff Dieffenbach, Michelle LaBorde, Geoff Horsfall, Karen Butler, Jill Stanko, Sherri Rowe, Kay Power, and Rob Carson. Special thanks are due to Toni Backstrom, who manages the LETRS program with enthusiasm, competence, and flare, and Steve Mitchell, the publisher of LETRS.

About the Authors

Louisa C. Moats, Ed.D., is a nationally recognized authority on reading instruction, how children learn to read, why many people have trouble reading, and treatment of reading problems. Louisa has been a neuropsychology technician, teacher, graduate school instructor, licensed psychologist, researcher, conference speaker, and author. She spent 15 years in private practice in Vermont, specializing in evaluation of and consultation with individuals of all ages who experienced difficulty with reading, spelling, writing, and oral language. After advising the California Reading Initiative for one year, Louisa was site director of the NICHD Early Interventions Project in Washington, D.C., a four-year project that included daily work with inner-city teachers and children. Recently, she has devoted herself to the improvement of teacher training and professional development.

Louisa earned her bachelor's degree at Wellesley College, her master's degree at Peabody College of Vanderbilt, and her doctorate in reading and human development from the Harvard Graduate School of Education. She was licensed to teach in three states before undertaking her doctoral work. In addition to LETRS®, Louisa has authored and coauthored books, including:

* *Speech to Print: Language Essentials for Teachers* (Moats, 2010)
* *Basic Facts About Dyslexia & Other Reading Problems* (Moats & Dakin, 2008)
* *Parenting a Struggling Reader* (Hall & Moats, 2002)
* *Straight Talk About Reading* (Hall & Moats, 1998)
* *Spelling: Development, Disability, and Instruction* (Moats, 1995)

Instructional materials include *Spellography* (Moats & Rosow, 2003) and *Primary Spelling by Pattern, Level 1* (Javernick & Moats, 2008) and *Level 2* (Hooper & Moats, 2011).

Louisa's many journal articles, book chapters, and policy papers include the American Federation of Teachers' *Teaching Reading Is Rocket Science*. In 2010, she contributed to the development of the Common Core State Standards in English Language Arts for the National Governors Association and Council of Chief State School Officers.

Carrie Hancock, Ph.D., is a 2002 graduate of the University of Oregon School Psychology Program where she studied and conducted research with Drs. Mark Shinn, Roland Good, and Ruth Kaminski. Dr. Hancock worked for the Arizona Department of Education as the program director for early reading assessment. She coordinated all *DIBELS®*-related training, follow-up, materials development, and technical support for the state of Arizona, including 72 Reading First Grant recipients.

Prior to her career at the Arizona Department of Education, Dr. Hancock worked as a school psychologist for three years assisting schools in implementing *DIBELS* schoolwide within comprehensive reading programs. She has conducted numerous local, state, and national presentations on effective early literacy instruction and implementing *DIBELS* within a Response to Intervention model.

Currently, Dr. Hancock is an educational consultant providing support to schools, school districts, and state departments around the country.

Contents

Chapter 2 Who Needs Help? Interpreting Screening Measures

Chapter 3 What Kind of Help Is Needed? The Subtypes of Reading Difficulty

Chapter 4   Is the Help Helping?

Chapter 5 Schoolwide Implementation of Data-Based Intervention

Introduction to LETRS®

LETRS® (*Language Essentials for Teachers of Reading and Spelling*) is professional development for educators who are responsible for improving K–12 instruction in reading, writing, and spelling. The content of LETRS is delivered in a series of 12 core modules in book format. Each module in the series focuses on one topic, with the topics aligned to be delivered in sequential training. Thus, one book for use in the course of training—and later as a professional reference—is provided for each module. Each module is typically delivered in a one- to two-day presentation by a national, regional, or local district trainer who has met the LETRS trainer certification guidelines developed by Dr. Moats and her colleagues.

module [mŏjūl] n.
a self-contained component of a whole that is used in conjunction with, and has a well-defined connection to, the other components

LETRS modules are used for both in-service training and for undergraduate and graduate courses in reading and literacy. They can also be resources for any educator charged with improving the language skills of students. LETRS is designed so that participants will understand:

1. *How* children learn to read and *why* some children have difficulty with this aspect of literacy;
2. *What* must be taught during reading and spelling lessons and *how to teach* most effectively;
3. *Why* all components of reading instruction are necessary and *how* they are related;
4. *How to interpret* individual differences in student achievement; and
5. *How to explain* the form and structure of English.

LETRS modules are designed to be delivered in sequence, but flexible sequencing is possible. In sequence, the modules build on overview concepts and introductory content, and then on phonology, phoneme awareness, and the writing system (orthography) of English (Modules 1–3). Next, the modules progress to topics in vocabulary, fluency, and comprehension instruction (Modules 4–6). Later modules (7–9) target reading instruction for the primary grades and include this module on assessment for prevention and early intervention. The final series (Modules 10–12), designed for educators who work with students at grade 3 and above, addresses advanced phonics and word study, comprehension and study skills in content-area reading, and assessment of older students.

A presenter CD-ROM (developed by Dr. Carol Tolman) accompanies each LETRS module, providing a PowerPoint® presentation that supports, extends, and elaborates module content.

The presentation slides are designed to be used by professional development personnel, higher education faculty, consultants, reading specialists, and coaches who have a strong background in the concepts and who have been trained and certified to present LETRS.

LETRS is not a reading instruction program, and LETRS modules do not substitute for program-specific training. Rather, LETRS complements and supports the implementation of programs aligned with scientifically based reading research (SBRR). A complete approach to improving reading instruction must include: (a) selection and use of core and supplemental instructional materials; (b) professional development on how to use the materials; (c) professional development that leads to broader understandings; (d) classroom coaching and in-school supports; (e) an assessment program for data-based problem-solving; and (f) strong leadership. A comprehensive, systemic approach with these elements will support a Response to Intervention (RtI) initiative.

We recommend that teachers who have had little experience with or exposure to the science of reading and research-based practices begin with LETRS *Foundations* (Glaser & Moats, 2008). *Foundations* is a stepping stone into the regular LETRS modules. Other related resources have been developed to support LETRS professional development, including:

- LETRS Interactive CD-ROMs for Modules 2, 3, 4, 7, and 8 (developed with a grant from the Small Business Innovation Research [SBIR] program of the National Institute of Child Health and Human Development [NICHD]), which provide additional content and skill practice for topics often considered challenging to implement and teach in the classroom.
- *The Reading Coach: A How-To Manual for Success* (Hasbrouck & Denton, 2005)
- *Teaching English Language Learners: A Supplementary* LETRS® *Module* (Argüelles, Baker, & Moats, 2011)
- LETRS *for Early Childhood Educators* (Paulson & Moats, 2010)
- *Teaching Reading Essentials* (Moats & Farrell, 2007), a series of video demonstrations used extensively by LETRS trainers throughout the delivery of training.

The chart on the next page represents a fundamental idea in LETRS—that language systems underlie reading and writing, and students' difficulties with reading and writing are most effectively addressed if the structures and functions of language are taught to them directly. We ask teachers to learn the terminology of language systems and to recognize that language is an important common denominator that links reading with writing, speaking, and listening comprehension.

Content of LETRS Modules Within the Language-Literacy Connection

Components of Comprehensive Reading Instruction	Organization of Language						
	Phonology	Morphology	Orthography	Semantics	Syntax	Discourse and Pragmatics	Etymology
Phonological Awareness	2	2					
Phonics, Spelling, and Word Study	3, 7	3, 7, 10	3, 7, 10				3, 10
Fluency	5	5	5	5	5		
Vocabulary	4	4	4	4	4		4
Text Comprehension		6		6	6	6, 11	
Written Expression			9, 11	9, 11	9, 11	9, 11	
Assessment	8, 12	8, 12	8, 12	8, 12	8, 12	8, 12	

Note: Numbers represent individual modules in the LETRS series.

Knowledge and Practice Standards for Teachers in Assessment of Reading

The following standards for teacher preparation in the area of assessment of reading difficulties are excerpted from the International Dyslexia Association's (IDA) *Knowledge and Practice Standards for Teachers of Reading* (http://www.interdys.org). The content of LETRS Module 8 is guided by two sets of IDA standards, the first of which summarizes what teachers should know in the area of early assessment of reading, spelling, and writing:

1. Understand the differences among screening, diagnostic, outcome, and progress-monitoring assessments.

2. Understand basic principles of test construction, including reliability, validity, and norm-referencing, and know the most well-validated screening tests designed to identify students at risk for reading difficulties.

3. Understand the principles of progress-monitoring and the use of graphs to indicate progress.

4. Know the range of skills typically assessed by diagnostic surveys of phonological skills, decoding skills, oral reading skills, spelling, and writing.

5. Recognize the content and purposes of the most common diagnostic tests used by psychologists and educational evaluators.

6. Interpret measures of reading comprehension and written expression in relation to an individual student's component profile.

The second set of IDA standards summarizes what teachers should be able to do when they use assessments with students:

1. Match each type of assessment and its purpose.
2. Match examples of technically adequate, well-validated screening, diagnostic, outcome, and progress-monitoring assessments.
3. Using case study data, accurately interpret progress-monitoring graphs to decide whether or not a student is making adequate progress.
4. Using case study data, accurately interpret subtest scores from diagnostic surveys to describe a student's patterns of strengths, weaknesses, and instructional needs.
5. Find and interpret appropriate print and electronic resources for evaluating tests.
6. Using case study data, accurately interpret a student's performance on reading comprehension or written expression measures and make appropriate instructional recommendations.

Overview of Module 8

The focus of Module 8 is screening, diagnosing, and monitoring the instructional needs of students in grades K–3 who are showing signs of risk. The purpose of these activities is early identification and intervention to minimize reading failure at these early levels, and progress-monitoring to determine Response to Intervention (RtI). We present a general strategy for selecting and using assessments for specific purposes. Interpretation of classroom screening results and individual students' diagnostic assessments is explored through case studies that represent a range of student subtypes or profiles, including those with decoding and phonological processing weaknesses, orthographic processing or fluency problems, and/or oral and written language comprehension difficulties. Assessment results are linked to appropriate instructional methods, goals, and programs.

Chapter 1

Early Intervention and RtI

Learner Objectives for Chapter 1

- Understand why early intervention is critical for preventing reading problems.
- Describe and distinguish the purposes of four kinds of assessments (outcome, screening, diagnostic, and progress-monitoring).
- Understand the basic tenets of an RtI (Response to Intervention) problem-solving model.

Warm-Up: True or False?

- Are these statements true or false?

	TRUE	FALSE
1. We can predict silent passage-reading comprehension in third-graders fairly well using simple screening tests of speech-sound awareness and letter knowledge in kindergarten.		
2. Many children who seem behind in reading readiness at the kindergarten level are late bloomers; if we wait a year or two, they will grow out of their problems.		
3. A 45-minute screening in kindergarten will be more reliable than a 10–15-minute screening for predicting long-term outcomes in reading.		
4. Most reading problems emerge late, around the end of third grade, when students must shift from learning to read to reading to learn.		
5. Once we know a student's level or "tier" of reading growth, we will know what kind of instruction he/she needs.		

Preventing Reading Failure

The road to reading success begins early in life. Early experiences with language stimulation, books, and the world outside home help predict how likely it is that a child will succeed in school. Early literacy experiences, however, do not explain why students with good preschool preparation succumb to reading failure, or why students with poor preschool preparation can defy the odds and learn to read and write very well. While literacy does, in part, depend on a supportive environment in which reading is valued, modeled, and practiced, learning to read requires more than a literacy-oriented environment and exposure to books at home. For many, early reading depends on instruction and practice that involve sustained effort over a few years.

The premise that children can be "late bloomers" has been popular in education for decades. Think of the practices that reflect this assumption: we debate age cut-offs for entry into school; we screen children for overall "readiness" and "maturity"; and we retain students who are not on grade level, hoping that "another year" will fix their problems. Traditionally, we have waited until the end of third grade to refer students for special education evaluations (Finn, Rotherham, & Hokanson, 2001) if they have failed to improve for several years and the "developmental lag" hypothesis has not panned out.

Researchers who have followed children's reading development from kindergarten onward, however, have cast serious doubts on the "developmental lag" hypothesis. Once children are behind—which happens very early in the game—they do not catch up unless intervention is intensive, timely, and well-informed. Connie Juel (1988), for example, followed the growth of 54 children in a Texas school between first and fourth grades. She showed that students who were in the lowest quartile (below the 25th percentile) on an end-of-year reading test in first grade had a .88 probability of being in the lower quartile at the end of fourth grade. The probability that a good reader in first grade would become a poor reader in fourth grade was .12—very low. Juel concluded that once a poor reader, almost always a poor reader, given "business as usual" in the classroom.

On a larger scale, the Connecticut Longitudinal Study (Francis, Shaywitz, Stuebing, Shaywitz, & Fletcher, 1996; Shaywitz et al., 1999) followed about 400 randomly selected kindergarten students from a broad sample of communities across the state and followed them to the end of high school, administering an extensive battery of individual tests each year. Between grades 1 and 9, students who started out in the bottom 25 percent (the lowest one-quarter) of reading achievement remained there for the duration of the study, with very few exceptions. All students tended to reach a plateau in their reading growth at about sixth grade, and the gap between good and poor readers was never closed. Other large-scale, scientifically conducted research (Mehta, Foorman, Branum-Martin, & Taylor, 2005; Olson, 2004) has found that children at risk for reading problems are very likely to end up where they start out, relative to other students, unless intensive intervention counteracts this prediction.

The Science of Prediction

The longitudinal studies just cited showed not only that students who start out behind tend to stay behind, but also that most poor readers have specific skill deficits that can be quickly and easily measured and treated before they balloon into chronic, serious reading and writing delays.

At the kindergarten level, even before children have learned to read, those who will be poor readers almost invariably lack the foundational skills necessary to learn to read. These skills include knowledge of letter names, awareness of speech sounds (i.e., phonemes and other word parts), the ability to match phonemes to graphemes, the ability to write letters, and knowledge of word meanings. These skill deficits get in the way of learning to decode words, use phonics, and establish automatic ("sight") word recognition. Sometimes these skills are lacking because the child has had no opportunity to learn them, and sometimes the skills are lacking because of a constitutional—and often genetically influenced—predisposition to reading and/or learning difficulty.

The reason that these fundamental problems predict silent-reading comprehension at the end of third grade is that less-skilled readers will be slow and inaccurate from the start. They will make many errors as they try to recognize printed words. As a consequence, they will read far fewer words accurately and receive far less exposure to words that they need to learn. Instead of developing automatic "sight" recognition of thousands of words—like a good reader who has read many more pages of text—they will slog through print and get much less exposure to words and information (Cunningham & Stanovich, 1998).

Instead of building associations that link phonemes, graphemes, and word meanings, as well as consolidating those associations into accurate and detailed whole-word images in memory, the poor reader will store inaccurate or incomplete word images in memory, and thus be more likely to make errors in both printed word recognition and spelling. These problems, in turn, engender a domino effect of limitations: they limit the development of reading fluency, which limits text exposure, which limits vocabulary and knowledge acquisition, which limits comprehension (Torgesen, Rashotte, & Alexander, 2001; Torgesen, 2004). *Figure 1.1* represents the consequences of getting off to a poor start in reading.

Figure 1.1   The Natural History of Early Reading Difficulty

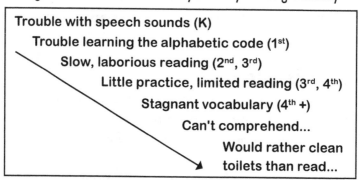

Trouble with speech sounds (K)
Trouble learning the alphabetic code (1st)
Slow, laborious reading (2nd, 3rd)
Little practice, limited reading (3rd, 4th)
Stagnant vocabulary (4th +)
Can't comprehend...
Would rather clean toilets than read...

The cascading effects of poor basic reading skills continue as the student moves along through the grades. Students who find that reading is difficult must expend much more energy than a good reader to accomplish the same assignment. The required effort taxes motivation and persistence. Reading and writing can be frustrating and unrewarding, and many students bail out early, before they have learned to read for pleasure or for information. They are lost by the intermediate or middle grades, casualties of a process that began even before they set foot in school.

The good news in this otherwise bleak story is that we now know much better how to identify at-risk students before failure has set in, and we have evidence that certain approaches to instruction can address early reading problems quite effectively. We do not have to wait months or years before we intervene to prevent the "nasty downward spiral" (Torgesen, 2004). This is possible because many researchers have worked diligently for years to establish a science of prediction and to outline what to do with students at risk.

The realization that reading skill is necessary for school success and that basic reading problems can be prevented and ameliorated if they are caught early has driven many state and federal reading initiatives. Important research reviews (Armbuster, Lehr, & Osborn, 2001; National Reading Panel, 2000; Rayner, Foorman, Perfetti, Pesetsky, & Seidenberg, 2001; Snow, Burns, & Griffin, 1998), policy statements (American Federation of Teachers, 1999), and legislation (Reading Excellence Act, 1998; Reading First, No Child Left Behind, 2001) have promoted early identification and intervention with students in the "basic" and "below basic" categories of reading achievement. Those reviews led to a significant change in the reauthorization of the Individuals with Disabilities Education Act of 2004, allowing states and districts to use a portion of special education funds for early intervention and to measure students' response to instruction before they were qualified for special services.

Our discussion of the rationale and methods of early intervention will begin with delineation of four types of assessments and their uses. In this chapter, we also discuss the origin and intent of Response to Intervention (RtI) initiatives. We end the chapter with an outline of a multistage approach that will use all four kinds of assessment.

Four Types of Assessments

Four types of assessments are described and contrasted in this section:
- Outcome
- Screening
- Progress-Monitoring
- Diagnostic

These four kinds of assessments are widely acknowledged in federal and state policies, guidelines, and standards. All of them should be used in a comprehensive approach to assessment. Each has unique purposes and characteristics.

Outcome Assessments

Outcome, or summative, assessments are "high-stakes," end-of-year accountability tests, currently administered by most states. Compliance with the provisions of the No Child Left Behind legislation has required administration of these tests, although state standards for "passing" rates have been varied and controversial. Outcome tests are distinguished by the following characteristics:

- All students are assessed within a narrow time frame (e.g., a week or a few days) once per year in groups.
- Tests have time limits and are proctored.
- Silent, independent reading is assessed.
- Passage-reading comprehension is the major (and sometimes the only) focus.
- Scores are reported as standard scores, percentiles, and normal curve equivalents (see *Figure 1.2*, next page) so that consumers can tell where an individual stands in relation to normative data for that age group or grade level.
- States may develop their own assessment or use a test that is nationally normed.

Figure 1.2 The Bell Curve, or Normal Curve

Percentage of cases in 8 portions of the curve	.13%	2.14%	13.59%	34.13%	34.13%	13.59%	2.14%	.13%
Standard Deviations	-4σ	-3σ	-2σ	-1σ	0	+1σ	+2σ	+3σ	+4σ
Cumulative Percentages		0.1%	2.3%	15.9%	50%	84.1%	97.7%	99.9%	
Percentiles				1 5 10 20 30 40 50 60 70 80 90 95 99					
Z scores	-4.0	-3.0	-2.0	-1.0	0	+1.0	+2.0	+3.0	+4.0
T scores		20	30	40	50	60	70	80	
Standard Nine (Stanines)		1	2 3 4 5 6 7 8					9	
Percentage in Stanine		4%	7% 12% 17% 20% 17% 12% 7%					4%	

The curved line represents the normal distribution of reading achievement scores in the population as a whole. The midpoint (0) is the average score (50th percentile); 1 standard deviation above and below average will encompass 34% of the distribution to either side of average, or the interval of the 16th percentile to the 84th percentile. Between the 1st and 2nd standard deviation is another 14% of the population, or the interval between the 2nd percentile and the 98th percentile.

State initiatives and those funded with federal funds (e.g., Title I and School Improvement Grants) usually require districts to demonstrate improvement with students at risk. End-of-year tests (e.g., the Stanford-10, Iowa Test of Basic Skills, Terra Nova, and Metropolitan Achievement Tests) are often used for this purpose. Outcome test results are usually reported separately (disaggregated) by subgroup, such as age, gender, socioeconomic status, special education status, or race. Accountability systems often rely on such tests to show overall progress within a state, district, or school. Many states—including California, Florida, Texas, and Colorado—have developed their own outcome achievement measures. These have been criticized for lack of consistent alignment with each other or with a national standard such as the National Assessment of Educational Progress, so results are difficult to compare across states. These realities have led to widespread support for the *Common Core State Standards*, developed in 2010 by the National Governor's Association and the Council of Chief State School Officers, which in turn will provide a framework for a national assessment.

Outcome tests given by districts and states reflect the end result of curriculum design, program implementation, and individual teachers' efforts over the course of an entire school year. The limitation of these tests, of course, is that by the end of third or fourth grade (when the summative tests are usually given), it is too late to plan and implement a more effective instructional program without considerable cost and effort. Educators should know much earlier who is at risk and should be directing resources to those students—not only because it is easier to get results with early intervention, but also because students who have failed for several years to "catch on" to reading may be very frustrated and pessimistic. Intervention with older students takes much more time and is much more expensive and difficult to implement than early intervention with kindergarten and first-grade students (Torgesen et al., 2001). Schools can and should know how many students are likely to meet state standards far in advance of the spring date on which the high-stakes tests are given.

Screening Assessments

Screening supported by research

Following decades of research, several screening instruments now exist that have been administered to very large populations of students and studied in depth for their ability to flag students who are likely to fail their state's outcome test. The most well validated and widely used screening instruments include:

- *DIBELS*® (6th ed.) and *DIBELS*® *Next* (Dynamic Indicators of Basic Early Literacy Skills)
  Web site: https://dibels.uoregon.edu or http://www.soprislearning.com
- *AIMSweb*®
  Web site: http://www.AIMSweb.com
- *TPRI* (Texas Primary Reading Inventory)
  Web site: http://www.tpri.org
- *PALS*™ (Phonological Awareness Literacy Screening)
  Web site: http://www.pals.virginia.edu
- *FAIR* (Florida Assessments for Instruction in Reading) (Florida Department of Education, 2009)
- *CPAA* (Children's Progress Academic Assessment)
  Web site: http://www.childrensprogress.com
- *IDEL*® (Indicadores Dinámicos del Éxito en la Lectura)
  Web site: https://dibels.uoregon.edu/idelinfo.php or http://www.soprislearning.com
- *Tejas LEE* (El Inventario de Lectura en Español de Tejas)
  Web site: http://www.tpri.org

Screening assessments such as *DIBELS* are designed to identify at-risk students efficiently and effectively *before they fail or before they establish a pattern of failure.* Such measures are intended to martial resources for instruction that would otherwise be spent on more testing. Early identification of reading problems is possible because the scores on screening measures indicate who is most likely to pass the high-stakes, outcome tests given at the end of each grade. Screening instruments are designed to be:

- administered to all students individually at least three times per school year in the early grades;
- brief (10–15 minutes per student);
- efficient and cost-effective; and
- a rough indicator of mild, moderate, and severe risk in basic reading skills.

A new definition of "grade level" is necessary to interpret the results of screening measures. Grade level on predictive screening assessment is a *minimal proficiency target* that *predicts* a passing score on the high-stakes outcome test. Over and over, studies continue to find that the appropriate "benchmark" target is equivalent to about the 40th percentile. A screening test can tell us how likely it is that a student will pass the high-stakes, group-administered achievement test given at the end of the school year, but it does not tell us with great precision how that student compares to others in the normative sample.

Screening is an exercise in narrowing probabilities so that better instructional decisions can be made. *Figure 1.3* represents the proportion of students who are deemed "at risk" nationally.

Figure 1.3   Proportion of Students at Risk for Reading Difficulty

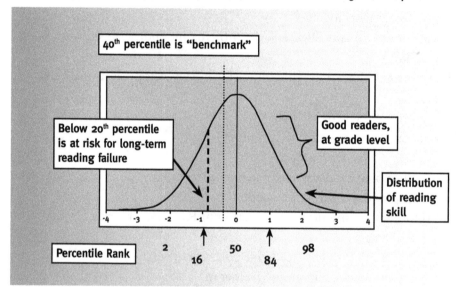

In kindergarten and first grade, screening tests are usually focused on measurement of "simple" skills that underlie word recognition. Most screening subtests are timed, and the results, therefore, are affected by both accuracy and speed. Screening tests measure the word recognition component of reading development and, through timed oral-passage reading, the comprehension component of Scarborough's (2001) rope model referred to throughout LETRS and reproduced in *Figure 1.4*.

Figure 1.4 The Reading Rope
(Scarborough, 2001, p. 98)

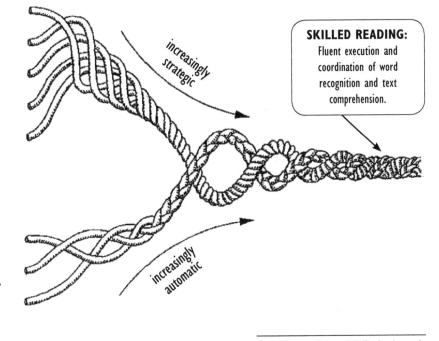

LANGUAGE COMPREHENSION

BACKGROUND KNOWLEDGE
(facts, concepts, etc.)

VOCABULARY
(breadth, precision, links, etc.)

LANGUAGE STRUCTURES
(syntax, semantics, etc.)

VERBAL REASONING
(inference, metaphor, etc.)

LITERACY KNOWLEDGE
(print concepts, genres, etc.)

WORD RECOGNITION

PHONOLOGICAL AWARENESS
(syllables, phonemes, etc.)

DECODING (alphabetic principle,
spelling-sound correspondences)

SIGHT RECOGNITION
(of familiar words)

increasingly strategic

increasingly automatic

SKILLED READING:
Fluent execution and coordination of word recognition and text comprehension.

Used with permission of Hollis Scarborough.

Typically, the following skills are briefly sampled in screening instruments because they do the best job in explaining or predicting variation in overall reading proficiency at the end of grade 3:

- Letter naming
- Phoneme segmentation
- Letter-sound correspondence
- Real-word reading (out of context)
- Nonsense-word reading
- Spelling by sound
- Oral passage reading fluency (after mid-first grade) with retelling
- Maze passage reading (third grade and beyond)

We will take a closer look at some specific measures in Chapter 2 of this module, but at this point, it is important to recognize that the lower strands of the rope are most often measured in screening tests.

Sometimes, screening measures like *DIBELS* are criticized because they do not appear to assess comprehension and more "authentic" reading skills very thoroughly. We believe, however, that the measurement of foundational reading skills in screening tests is justified by the following, well-established facts:

- Fluent reading is not possible without accurate, efficient word recognition (Rayner et al., 2001; Stanovich, 2000).
- Students with poor reading skills are distinguished by weaknesses in phonological processing, or awareness of the speech-sound structures in spoken language (see *Figure 1.5,* next page).

Figure 1.5 Profiles of Reading Disabilities
Reprinted with permission from Fletcher, Lyon, Fuchs, & Barnes (2007, p. 46)

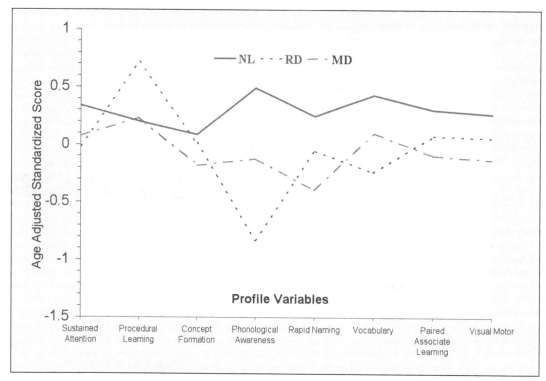

Profiles of reading disabled (RD) (lowest 30%) students on cognitive tests, compared to normal learners (NL) and students with mathematics disabilities (MD). Low scores on phonological awareness measures distinguish those with reading difficulties.

- "Simple" tasks predict reading comprehension very well up to third grade, especially if the measures reflect accuracy and speed (Good, Simmons, & Kame'enui, 2001; Schatschneider, Fletcher, Francis, Carlson, & Foorman, 2004).
- Screening is only the first step in implementation of differentiated instruction. Some students learn to recognize words easily and need less teacher-directed, code-oriented instruction. At-risk students will need more explicit, systematic teaching and practice to progress (Aaron, Joshi, Boulware-Gooden, & Bentum, 2008; Al Otaiba et al., 2009; Connor, Morrison, & Katch, 2004).
- Screening should be brief, or its purpose is defeated. Screening that takes too long detracts from valuable instructional time.
- Oral reading fluency overlaps with or explains reading comprehension test results from mid-first to end of third grade. By fifth grade, verbal reasoning, vocabulary, and background knowledge become more and more important to overall reading achievement (Buck & Torgesen, 2003; Speece, 2005). Oral reading fluency, then, is a valuable indicator of overall reading proficiency in primary-grade students.

Two studies that are typical of scientific research providing evidence for the power of early screening are summarized here.

Research Abstract

Boscardin, C. K., Muthén, B., Francis, D. J., & Baker, E. L. (2008). Early identification of reading difficulties using heterogeneous developmental trajectories. *Journal of Educational Psychology, 100(*1), 192–208.

Serious conceptual and procedural problems associated with current diagnostic methods call for alternative approaches to assessing and diagnosing students with reading problems. This study presents a new analytic model to improve the classification and prediction of children's reading development. Growth mixture modeling was used to identify the presence of 10 different heterogeneous developmental patterns. In all, 411 children in kindergarten through Grade 2 from 3 elementary schools in Texas were administered measures of phonological awareness, word recognition, and rapid naming skills four times a year. The mean ages were 5.8 years (SD = 0.35) for the kindergartners, 6.9 years (SD = 0.39) for Grade 1, and 8.0 years (SD = 0.43) for Grade 2; the percentage of boys was 50%. The results indicate that precursor reading skills such as phonological awareness and rapid naming are highly predictive of word reading (word recognition) and that developmental profiles formed in kindergarten are directly associated with development in Grades 1 and 2. Students identified as having reading-related difficulties in kindergarten exhibited slower development of word recognition skills in subsequent years of the study.

Research Abstract

Schatschneider, C., Fletcher, J. M., Francis, D. J., Carlson, C. D., & Foorman, B. R. (2004). Kindergarten prediction of reading skills: A longitudinal comparative analysis. *Journal of Educational Psychology, 96(*2), 265–282.

There is considerable focus in public policy on screening children for reading difficulties. Sixty years of research have not resolved questions of what constructs assessed in kindergarten best predict subsequent reading outcomes. This study assessed the relative importance of multiple measures obtained in a kindergarten sample for the prediction of reading outcomes at the end of first and second grades. Analyses revealed that measures of phonological awareness, letter-sound knowledge, and naming speed consistently accounted for the unique variance across reading outcomes, whereas measures of perceptual skills and oral language and vocabulary did not. These results show that measures of letter name and letter sound knowledge, naming speed, and phonological awareness are good predictors of multiple reading outcomes in Grades 1 and 2.

Limitations of screening measures

What about students whose main problems occur in the comprehension strands of the "reading rope" model? Those students may have low language proficiency, low verbal-reasoning skills, limited vocabularies, less experience with complex syntax found in written language, and/or limited background knowledge. So far, screening measures in areas such as vocabulary development and oral language comprehension have not been as available, as valid, or as reliable as those that measure word recognition and oral passage reading for fluency. These areas are much more difficult to sample briefly and reliably. They do not predict outcomes as well in the early stages of reading, but they become increasingly important by the intermediate and middle grades.

Strong word-reading skills and passage-reading fluency, however, are just as necessary for students with wide-ranging language problems as they are for students whose problems center specifically on word recognition. It is helpful to know at what points all students are in basic reading skill development, even though strong basic skills alone will not be sufficient to support advanced comprehension of complex text. Many other aspects of language, background knowledge, and reading comprehension skills and strategies must be addressed in instruction.

The application of basic reading skills to passage comprehension is extremely important to teach, even though comprehension is not measured well in screening tests. Screening should be limited in its goals for the sake of time and efficiency. Other approaches will be needed to assess students' language proficiency and comprehension beyond the brief screening measures typically used by schools.

Another limitation of many screening measures, including *DIBELS*, is that the cut-points usually designate a group of students who will pass the state outcome test even though they score in the "mildly at risk" or "strategic" range. That is, many students score below the desirable benchmark on oral reading fluency, but they are going to be adequate in overall reading skill. Potential poor readers are over-identified, caught in the safety net of the "strategic intervention" range. Researchers (Catts, Petscher, Schatschneider, Bridges, & Mendoza, 2009; Compton, Fuchs, Fuchs, & Bryant, 2006; Schatschneider et al., 2004) call those students "false positives." In order to identify 90 percent of those who will have genuine difficulty, the "benchmark" cut-point on the screening test is set high.

For example, the graph in *Figure 1.6* shows that third-grade students who read about 110 words correct per minute on the Test of Oral Reading Fluency (TORF) at the end of the school year (designated by the vertical line in the middle of the scale) were highly likely to pass the Oregon State Achievement Test (OSAT) at a designated passing score of 201 (represented by the horizontal line). Those students' data points are in the upper right quadrant of the graph. However, about half of the students in the "at-risk" category, who read below 110 words correct per minute (in the upper left quadrant of the graph) also passed the OSAT. These are the "false positives" that result from screening that has a conservative cut-off score to designate risk.

Figure 1.6 Relationship Between TORF and OSAT

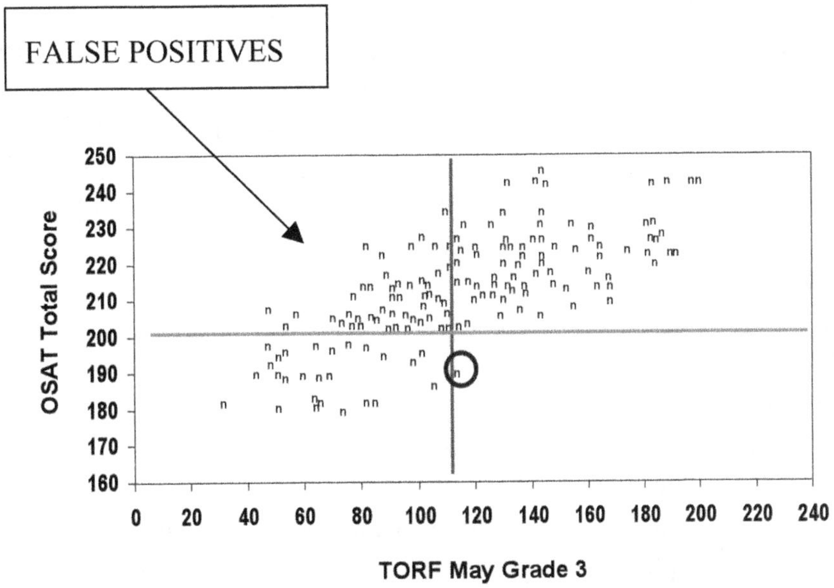

This figure shows the relationship between oral reading fluency (words correct per minute on the horizontal axis) and the likelihood of passing a state's year-end outcome measure in passage-reading comprehension. The upper left quadrant represents those students whose oral reading was below the cut-point but who passed the state test anyway—the "false positives."

Screening is, by nature, imprecise. Therefore, screening tests alone should not be the basis for determining who needs small-group instruction or what kind of instruction will help. Screening results should be checked against other sources of information, including teacher observations, a student's history, a student's classroom performance, and diagnostic surveys.

Teaching Tip

Screening tests measure only *some* of the essential aspects of instruction. What gets measured is not the same as what gets taught!

Progress-Monitoring Assessments

Progress-monitoring is necessary once students are found to be at risk and are placed in intervention programs or in intervention groups for several reasons. First, although we may know that a student is below a benchmark that predicts later success, we cannot know if instruction is working to close the gap unless we directly measure RtI. Second, insufficient response to instruction is one of the criteria by which students with learning disabilities can be identified under new rules for special education eligibility. Third, objective data is better than our subjective impressions or opinions of student progress. We are all biased observers.

Progress-monitoring assessments have the following characteristics:

- They are brief and measure progress toward a specific achievement goal.
- They have equivalent forms that allow for frequent administration.
- They are given frequently (every one to three weeks) to students who have been screened and placed in intervention groups.
- They are used to determine whether a given instructional program or approach is working to bring the student closer to a target or benchmark level of reading skill.

In *Figure 1.7*, a graph showing progress in oral reading fluency, the student made minimal progress for the first month of instruction (January of first grade). If something does not change, this student will not be on course to achieve the minimal benchmark of 40 words per minute by June of first grade. The instructional plan probably needs to be modified to ensure that this student gets on course and stays on course.

Figure 1.7 Progress-Monitoring Graph of a First-Grader

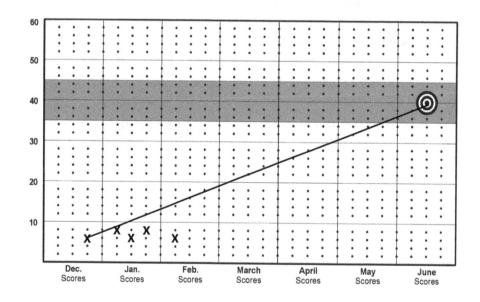

Diagnostic Assessments

The term **diagnostic assessment** has two meanings: First, it refers to the use of informal surveys and standardized tests that reveal in detail a student's academic knowledge and skill so that teachers can be specific in their instructional planning. Second, it refers to the activity of classifying a handicapping condition or disorder according to the diagnostic criteria established by a profession such as psychiatry or psychology. For example, "Dyslexia" and "Attention Deficit Hyperactivity Disorder" are diagnostic categories within the classification system used by psychologists and psychiatrists (DSM-V, the *Diagnostic and Statistical Manual of the American Psychiatric Association*).

Educational diagnostic assessments have the following characteristics:

- They are administered selectively to students at risk.
- They take more time than a screening test.
- They reveal detailed information about a student's mastery of a specific area of academic skill.
- They should be used to inform instruction and related aspects of treatment.

In this module, we will focus on learning to use a decoding skills survey and a spelling diagnostic survey. We will note the diagnostic instruments commonly used to assess other aspects of language and cognitive processing. In addition, we will focus on qualitative analysis of students' reading and writing as a way of gaining insight into the skills that students must be taught. Case studies will emphasize the use of multiple sources of information in decision-making.

Reliability, Validity, and Efficiency of Assessments

In order to be most useful in a school setting, assessments of any kind must meet certain psychometric criteria. The most important are reliability, validity, and efficiency.

- A *reliable* measure is likely to yield the same result if it were to be given several times on the same day in the same context.
- A *valid* measure is one that: (a) measures what it says it measures (construct validity); (b) corresponds well to other known, valid measures (concurrent validity); and (c) predicts with good accuracy how students are likely to perform on an accountability measure (predictive validity).
- An *efficient* measure can be given with relatively low cost in relatively little time, but the information gained is of substantial value.

The most important idea to remember is that all measures are imprecise to some extent. All contain what the test-makers refer to as "measurement error"; therefore, classification judgments about students should never be made on the basis of one measure alone. Multiple sources of information are best in making decisions about placements, groupings, instructional methods and programs, or student handicapping conditions. *Appendix A* includes longer, more detailed explanations about the realities of test construction and score interpretation.

Exercise 1.1 | Assessments You Use Now

- List the assessments that you and/or your school team use. Note whether they are helpful to you in grouping students and planning instruction. Compare notes with others in a small group.

Assessments	Very Helpful	Somewhat Helpful	Not Helpful
1. Outcome			
2. Screening			
3. Progress-monitoring			
4. Educational diagnostic			

Response to Intervention (RtI): A Preventive Approach

What Is RtI?

"RtI as a framework or model should be applied to decisions for general, remedial, and special education, creating a well-integrated system of instruction and intervention guided by student performance data that is close to the classroom."

—Judy Elliott, Chief Academic Officer, Los Angeles Unified School District

Response to Intervention (RtI) refers to a set of schoolwide procedures for organizing and delivering instruction that serves the following purposes:

1. Directing resources to *prevention and amelioration* of learning problems through early intervention.
2. *Unification and shared responsibility* for instructional outcomes across general education, remedial education, and special education.
3. *Identification* of students with learning disabilities, beyond the typical IQ-achievement discrepancy criterion.
4. *Implementation* of effective instruction and behavioral support for all students, regardless of classification.

In 2004, the United States Congress reauthorized funding for the Individuals with Disabilities Education Act (IDEA). This revision to the 1977 regulations states that:

a) states may not require a local education agency (LEA) to use a discrepancy model for determining whether a student has a learning disability;
b) states must permit the use of a process that determines if the student responds to scientific research-based intervention; and
c) states may permit other alternative research-based procedures for special education eligibility to be determined.

Why RtI?

The change in these rules moves systems away from reliance on time-consuming, expensive, difficult, and (often) instructionally irrelevant student evaluations to a focus on appropriate and timely instruction. Up to 15 percent of a school's special education funds can be used for providing preventive intervention—prior to referring students for special services. Students who may have learning disabilities can thus be distinguished from those who simply have not been taught or who have not had an opportunity to learn. Under these new rules, evidence must be obtained that appropriate instruction has been delivered through general education and data has been gathered showing the student's response to instruction before students receive special education services. Diagnostic testing and classification of learning disorders remains a part of the special education process, but students do not have to fail for months or years before they receive appropriate help.

When RtI models are successfully implemented (see, e.g., Brown-Chidsey & Steege, 2006), referrals to special education decrease, fewer students remain at risk, and schoolwide resources are used cooperatively for the benefit of all students.

Tiered Approaches to Organizing Instruction

RtI models have come to mean more than an alternative route to special education eligibility. RtI models rely on implementation of *multitiered* diagnostic and instructional systems. Under these policies, everyone in a school system has responsibility for the progress of all students. In fact, the most important purpose of RtI is to enhance the success of all students before special education services are relied upon to solve educational problems.

For an RtI system to work, six major factors are significant: (1) leadership; (2) curriculum and instruction; (3) school climate and culture; (4) a problem-solving process; (5) assessment; and (6) family and community involvement (Colorado Department of Education, 2008; Elliott, 2008). Problem-solving is organized around a few critical questions:

- Who needs help?
- Why do they need help?
- What kind of help do they need?
- Is the help helping?
- If not, what needs to be changed?

In order to answer these questions, the school system must be organized so that a range of curricular options, scheduling opportunities, and trained and available personnel are available. For example, Dr. Larry Tihen, Executive Director of Curriculum in Lee County, Fla., represents the curricular and instructional options available to his elementary and middle school staff illustrated in *Figure 1.8.*

Figure 1.8 RtI Delivery System
(Designed by Dr. Larry Tihen, Executive Director of Curriculum, Lee County, Fla.)

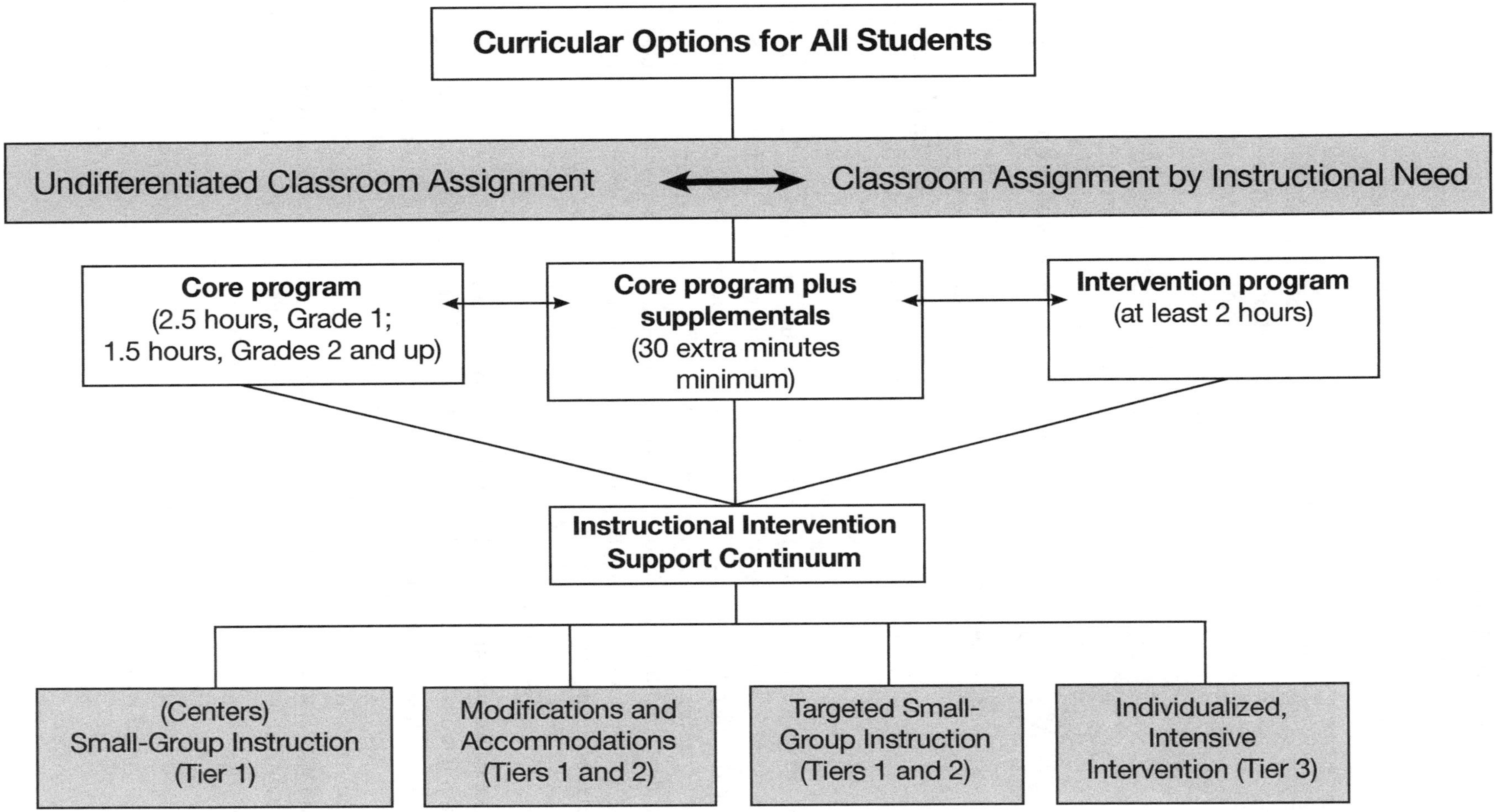

Curricular Options for All Students

Undifferentiated Classroom Assignment ⟷ Classroom Assignment by Instructional Need

Core program
(2.5 hours, Grade 1;
1.5 hours, Grades 2 and up)

Core program plus supplementals
(30 extra minutes minimum)

Intervention program (at least 2 hours)

Instructional Intervention Support Continuum

(Centers) Small-Group Instruction (Tier 1)

Modifications and Accommodations (Tiers 1 and 2)

Targeted Small-Group Instruction (Tiers 1 and 2)

Individualized, Intensive Intervention (Tier 3)

In an idealized schematic diagram, a three-tiered RtI system is often represented as an inverted pyramid (*Figure 1.9*).

Figure 1.9 Three Tiers of RtI Instruction

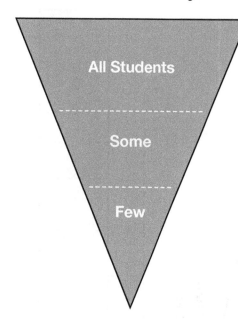

Tier 1: 75–80% of students respond to research-based, high-quality instruction, including differentiated small-group instruction.

Tier 2: 15–20% of students "at risk" receive targeted small-group instruction for 30 additional minutes. Some receive individual modifications and/or accommodations.

Tier 3: Approximately 5–10% of the most challenged students receive multiple supports and intensive intervention. They may be eligible for special education services.

In our experience, and in most schools that are implementing an RtI approach in order to focus on early intervention and prevention, the proportions of students who are considered "Tier 1," "Tier 2," and "Tier 3" vary according to the population served by the school. We believe the percentages in *Figure 1.9* are idealized because, in many schools, the proportion of students needing extra support exceeds 20 percent. If the proportion of students receiving small-group and specialized instruction is only 20 percent, the school staff is probably doing an exceptionally fine job.

Tier 1 instruction

Tier 1 instruction is that which the classroom teacher delivers, often with the support of paraprofessionals, reading coaches, or a grade-level team. In order to meet the needs of 70–80 percent of the students, a core curriculum must be well matched to the student population. A minimum of 2 hours daily (preferably 2.5 hours) should be devoted to classroom language arts instruction in first grade, and 1.5–2 hours in second and third grades. In schools or classes with underachieving students, even more time may be required. A well-designed core program, if implemented well, ensures that students build fluent word recognition skills and vocabulary, background knowledge, and comprehension abilities (National Reading Panel, 2000; Snow et al., 1998).

Classroom teachers in an RtI model will be involved in providing small-group, targeted instruction as well as whole-group instruction. Classroom teachers routinely gather screening and progress-monitoring data, participate in data-analysis meetings with a team, and collaborate to solve instructional problems.

What core program is best? All core programs have strengths and weaknesses. In schools where most students are at risk or below benchmark, the core programs should be selected to meet those students' characteristics. Those populations need more time on teacher-directed, systematic, code-based instruction and language development than students who are already at benchmark (Connor et al., 2004). Effective programs address all components every day, but the "balance" of components and instructional methodology may differ considerably in different settings.

Tier 2 instruction

Tier 2 instruction targets students who are in the lower 20–30 percent of the class. It is often given in small groups of about five well-matched students. Classroom teachers, trained paraprofessionals, learning specialists, reading teachers, and even administrative staff can work with small groups. Targeted intervention, usually designed for 30-minute lessons, is often given in addition to the core curriculum of Tier 1. Small-group instruction should be carefully designed to target areas of academic weakness that are determined by screening, diagnostic surveys, and progress-monitoring. Tier 2 instruction should also be coordinated with that in Tier 1. Some schools organize the entire school staff to provide small-group instruction at specific times during the day during a "walk to read" time.

Tier 3 instruction

Tier 3 usually refers to the intensive instruction, supports, and modifications necessary for students with the most severe reading, language, or writing disabilities. Very small-group (one to three students) instruction for well-matched students is delivered for as much as two hours daily to accelerate students' progress as much as possible. Alternative programs and curricula that employ special methodologies may be necessary. Often these programs require the teacher to have a high level of training. Tier 3 instruction may be delivered to students before they qualify for special education, within special education, or if they do not qualify for special education under discrepancy formulae.

Assessment is more frequent with Tier 3 students, since their rate of progress must be closely monitored. More far-ranging diagnostic assessments and multi-disciplinary evaluations are often indicated for these students, especially if they: (a) have obvious learning disabilities; (b) are referred for assessment by a teacher or parent; and/or (c) are not responding well to instruction.

Exercise 1.2 Where Are You and Your School With RtI?

- Check whether these features of an RtI model are being implemented where you work.

	Yes	No
1. A core comprehensive reading program is taught, completely and with fidelity, at least two hours per day.		
2. Approximately 75–80 percent of students are at benchmark or well above on screening tests.		
3. Small-group instruction and Centers are part of the regular classroom routine.		
4. Tier 2 instruction is given to small groups, constituted by instructional need, for an extra 30 minutes or more per day.		
5. Supplemental intervention is well-aligned with Tier 1 instruction.		
6. Screenings are efficient, reliable, and valid, and are given at least three times per school year to all kindergarten and grade 1 students.		
7. Progress-monitoring occurs at least once per month with Tier 2 students.		
8. The school schedule allows grade-level teams to meet regularly to discuss the screening and progress-monitoring data of all students.		
9. The school schedule is adjusted to allow sufficient, uninterrupted time for reading and language arts instruction at all tiers.		
10. Students with intensive instructional needs are identified early and placed in very small groups, where progress-monitoring is frequent.		
11. Optimal student success is being achieved with the current system.		

- With your colleagues, share what you see as the most pressing priorities for your school or school system in implementing RtI effectively.

_____

_____

Multistage, Strategic Assessment in an RtI Framework

All four kinds of assessments—outcome, screening, progress-monitoring, and diagnostic—are necessary to meet students' needs and to solve instructional problems in an RtI service delivery model. Throughout this LETRS module, we emphasize that multiple sources of information are important for answering these questions:

- Who needs help?
- Why do they need help?
- What kind of help do they need?
- Is the help helping?
- If not, what needs to be changed?

Figures 1.10 and *1.11* (next two pages) are flow charts that represent decision-making paths for the selection and use of assessments. In kindergarten and first grade (*Figure 1.10*), all students should be individually screened three times per school year. Those who are below benchmark on screening or who seem to be at risk should have additional diagnostic surveys of basic skills that will inform instruction. Tier 2 and Tier 3 students will be monitored as frequently as is appropriate.

In second and third grades (*Figure 1.11*), universal screening is still advised. Eventually, if teachers know students well and have a strong monitoring system in place, they may consider screening the strongest readers with a silent passage-reading test such as the Gates-MacGinitie® or with the state's outcome measure in reading, foregoing the individual screening process. The University of Virginia's *PALS*™ test, for example, identifies a range of proficient reading that exempts students from additional screening. Anyone who may be at risk, however, should be individually screened.

Both of the decision-making flow charts in *Figures 1.10* and *1.11* show that comprehension checks, formal and informal, are indicated when a student is a poor reader. In addition, some students may achieve benchmark levels on basic reading skills and oral reading, but may still have problems comprehending what they read. This profile is most likely when students are not proficient in English or when they have cognitive and affective disabilities that interfere with organized thinking or social awareness. Identification and description of comprehension problems will be discussed later in this module.

Figure 1.10 Decision-Making Model for Grades K–1

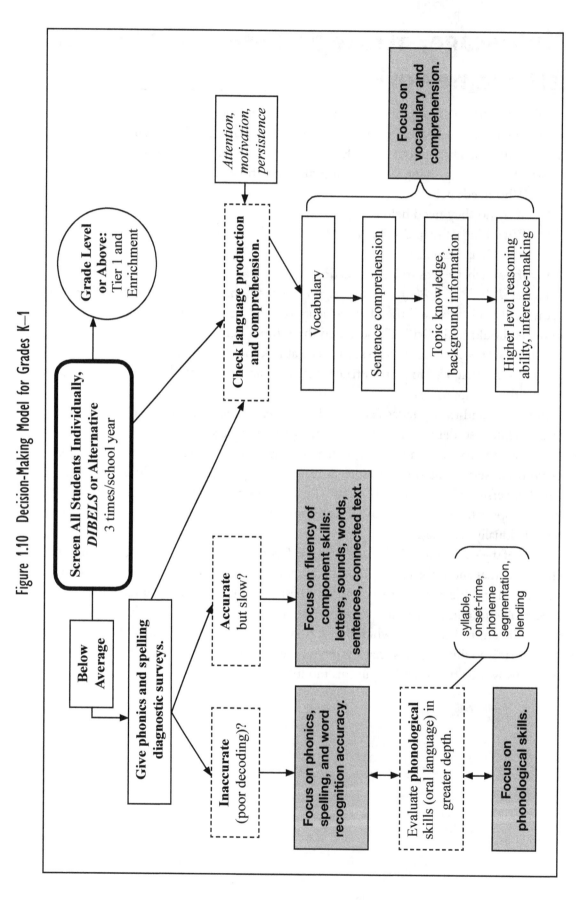

Figure 1.11 Decision-Making Model for Grades 2–3

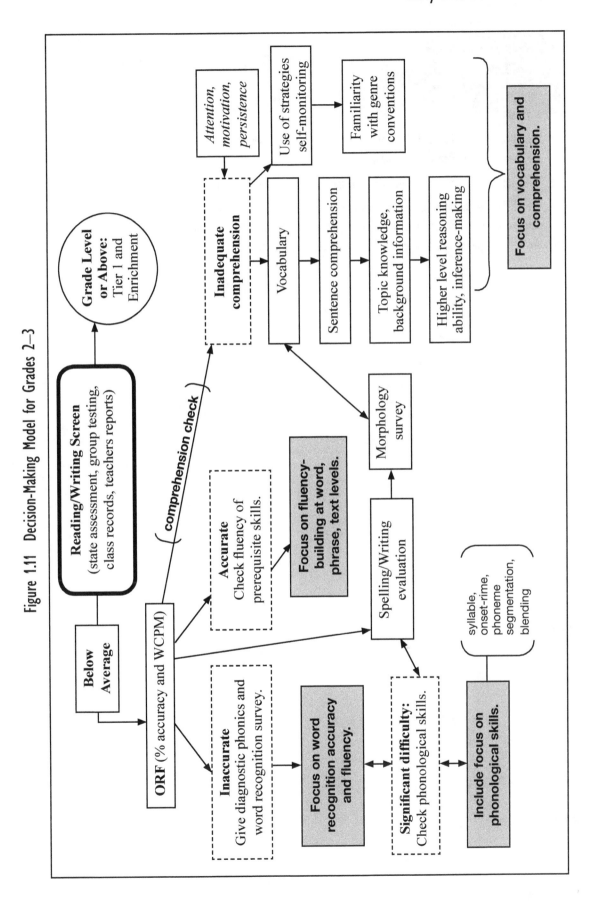

Exercise 1.3 Review and Compare Decision-Making Models

- Look over *Figures 1.10* and *1.11* (previous two pages) that depict the decisions involved in the selection, use, and interpretation of assessments.

- With your presenter, verbally describe the multistage assessment strategy that each figure represents.

- Even before we examine the various assessments in some depth, what is your reaction to the strategy as outlined in these charts? Does this look anything like the approach typically used in your school or district? We will ask you to revisit this question at the end of this module.

Chapter 2

Who Needs Help?
Interpreting Screening Measures

Learner Objectives for Chapter 2
- Know when and why universal screening is important.
- Be familiar with typical tasks in screening tests.
- Identify the component skill(s) and processes measured by various tasks.
- Interpret reports that classify students into levels of risk.

Warm-Up: A Short List of Questions
- Make a short list of questions about your students that you typically want answered when you are deciding what kind of instruction to provide to them.
- Next, sort the questions into those that you believe a screening measure can answer, and those a screening measure cannot (or should not) answer.

Why Use a Screening Measure?

Screening measures are typically given to all students at least three times per school year in kindergarten through third grade. Why? At these ages, growth in early reading skills is rapid, and students who are falling behind can be helped more easily than at any other age. Screenings at these critical intervals encourage pro-active intervention. Closing the gap between poor readers and good readers is easiest when problems are identified early (Mathes et al. 2005; Torgesen et al., 2001).

The charts in *Figures 2.1* and *2.2* (see next page), based on data from the University of Oregon (Good & Kaminski, 2003), show that students who are in the "at risk" category (the circles) fall behind early in first grade on single-word reading. The gap between those students and their peers widens steadily over time. Furthermore, by second grade, the group of students who were "at risk" at the end of first grade (the circles) do not spontaneously recover or catch up to their peers during their second-grade year. If students are behind in the first year or two, they are likely to stay behind unless very effective instruction can be implemented with sufficient frequency and intensity. The most open window for preventive intervention is kindergarten and first grade—and perhaps even earlier. Nevertheless, reading difficulties can be successfully treated in second grade (Connor, Morrison, & Underwood, 2007) and beyond (Calhoon, Sandow, & Hunter, 2010; Torgesen et al., 2001) if intervention is intensive enough and focused on teaching both language structure and comprehension.

Figure 2.1 First-Grade Students at Risk

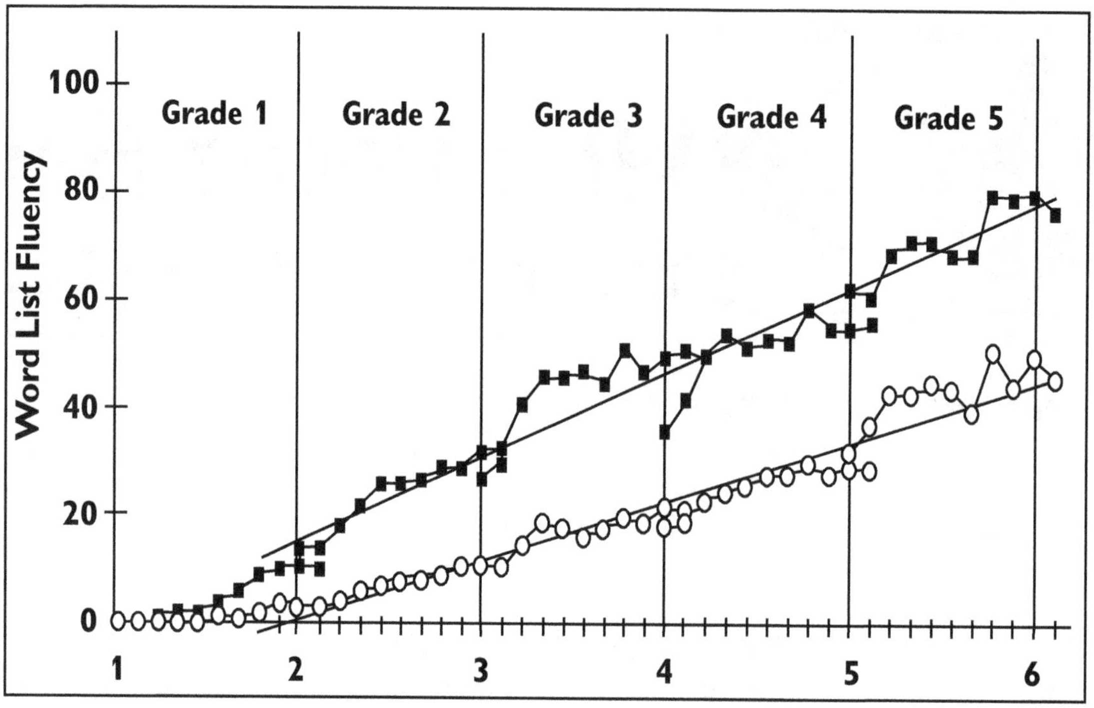

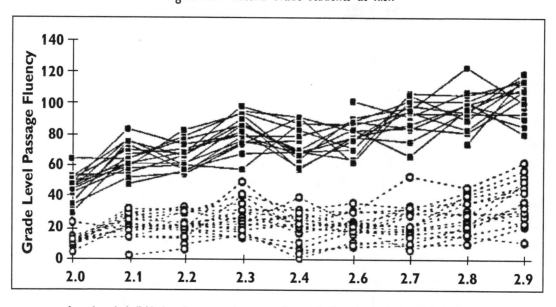

First-grade word recognition accuracy and fluency: Students at risk (circles), and students in the average range (squares).
Note the widening gap over time.

Figure 2.2 Second-Grade Students at Risk

Second-grade individual student scores in passage fluency: Students in the lowest 20 percent in the
beginning of the year (circles) and students progressing normally (squares), on month-by-month progress-monitoring.
Note that none of the students in the lower group spontaneously attain average achievement.

What Are the Advantages of Brief Screenings?

DIBELS®, AIMSweb®, TPRI, PALS™, FAIR, and similar measures are designed to take a student's "vital signs." Instead of doing a complete, time-consuming, and expensive evaluation after students have already failed, schools can carry out what Judith Dodson calls "reading triage" (Dodson, 2011). Students with mild difficulties can be flagged, and supportive instruction can be provided for them that will increase their likelihood of success.

Students with more severe difficulties or developmental disorders of learning and behavior can and should receive comprehensive evaluations without delay. Nevertheless, their reading problems can be flagged as early as possible, and they can be assigned to an intervention program even if the comprehensive evaluation is not yet complete. Just as blood pressure, cholesterol levels, pulse rate, weight gain or loss, and other easy-to-observe signs indicate general health in an adult, so do skill levels on simple measures indicate a student's overall reading health. The major, validated screening instruments have these advantages in common:

- They can save time and money otherwise spent on unnecessary, lengthy assessments.
- They are relatively simple to learn, administer, and score, especially with computerized data management systems.
- They are reliable and valid when given under standardized conditions.
- They may be repeated, with alternate forms, without loss of reliability.
- They provide a rough estimate of the degree of difficulty a student is experiencing.
- They focus a school on instruction and student progress.
- They enable early intervention when students may be most able to benefit.
- Reports can help with student-, classroom-, and school-level analyses of progress.

Exercise 2.1 | Compare Major Screening Instruments

- Look over this comparison chart of the most commonly used and extensively researched K–grade 3 screening measures and what they measure. If you use another assessment, identify the tasks or subtests on that measure.

- Keep in mind that even though the tasks from one screener to the next may have the same name or purport to measure the same skill, they may be somewhat different in the way they are administered (e.g., timed or untimed). Nevertheless, try to answer these questions:

1. Why do you think some tasks are very commonly used for screening?

    _____

2. Why might some tasks be used less commonly or appear in fewer screeners?

    _____

3. Why do you think that some tasks (e.g., "Word Use Fluency" in *DIBELS* 6th ed.) have been tried but are no longer used?

    _____

    _____

Task or Subtest	DIBELS Next	AIMSweb	FAIR	TPRI	PALS 1–3	(Your Choice)
Oral Reading Fluency	X	X	X	X	X	
Letter Naming	X	X	X	X	X	
First-Sound Segmentation Fluency	X					
Phoneme Segmentation (syllables)	X	X		X		
Phoneme Blending/Deletion			X		X	
Letter-Sound or Sound-Letter Correspondence		X	X	X	X	
Real-Word Reading Accuracy			X	X	X	
Nonsense-Word Reading Fluency	X			X		
Spelling/Word Building			X		X	
Maze Passage Comprehension	X	X	X			
Silent Reading Comprehension			X			
Retell Fluency	X					
Listening Comprehension			X	X		

If you guessed that the measures included in a screener are there because of their ability to predict reading outcomes, in combination with the others given at that grade level, you were on the right track. Other issues come into play as well. In order to understand how a screener is constructed, we must take a look at the research underlying the whole process of early reading screening.

The Research Behind *DIBELS* and Related Screening Measures

The Early Childhood Research Institute on Measuring Growth and Development (ECRI-MGD) at the University of Oregon has constructed, refined, and validated *DIBELS* on the basis of more than 25 years of research. The research has been funded mainly by the United States Department of Education (Good et al., 2001). Using data from many thousands of students across the United States, the research program has validated the relationships between the diagnostic indicators and end-of-year outcome measures. Further, the researchers have examined the construct validity of the measures; that is, the extent to which each measure quantifies what it says it is measuring, as well as the relationship between each measure and the overall recommendation regarding a student's risk category. The most recent revision of *DIBELS—DIBELS Next* (Good & Kaminski, 2010)—incorporates improvements that have been guided by validation studies. Technical reports summarizing the extensive research behind *DIBELS* are available from the University of Oregon's Web site (http://dibels. uoregon.edu).

DIBELS provided a template or start-point for other researchers working to improve screening and prediction of reading problems for early intervention. For example, the measurement technology underlying *DIBELS* was incorporated into the *AIMSweb* system. The *AIMSweb* system expanded the repertoire of measures of reading comprehension, spelling, and writing, and provided a completely web-based system of data analysis and reporting. The new *FAIR* (Florida Department of Education) assessment purports to improve on the predictive accuracy of *DIBELS* and *TPRI* and to measure reading skills in such a way that teachers will get more useful information about how to teach students in their classes. *DIBELS Next*, however, also includes new assessments, revised formats, and many improvements in the measures themselves. Various sophisticated products that build upon a quarter-century of scientific work are now on the market.

The measurement of Oral Reading Fluency (ORF) has a long history in research, beginning with the work of Stan Deno and Mark Shinn (Deno, Fuchs, Marston, & Shinn, 2001). A recurring finding in research is that automaticity of word reading and the fluency with which passages are read correlate very highly (.91) with success on traditional silent reading comprehension tests such as the Stanford Achievement Test (Fuchs, 2004; Fuchs, Fuchs, Hosp, & Jenkins, 2001; Wolf & Katzir-Cohen, 2001) up through third grade. A very high correlation between ORF and silent reading comprehension means that these measures overlap, or that they measure essentially the same thing: the combination of basic reading skill and passage reading comprehension. All of the brief, validated early screening measures include passages for measurement of oral reading fluency and recording of words correct per minute (WCPM).

In recent years, researchers at the University of Florida (Schatschneider et al., 2004), the University of Kansas (Catts et al., 2009), and Vanderbilt University (Compton et al., 2006) have critically examined the relative value of each type of screening indicator for prediction and progress-monitoring. Single indicators (e.g., phoneme segmentation or word list reading) are not as reliable or valid as combinations of several indicators. In addition, the relative importance of each indicator in a group of screening measures changes rapidly as reading skill develops. The combination of measures that best predict reading outcomes later on changes as students acquire reading skill, and there are trade-offs between efficiency (the time necessary to screen students) and predictive accuracy. "Reading" is a moving target; the skills that predict it change at each point in reading development, and researchers have to choose which combination of measures give them the best predictions in the least amount of time at a given grade level (Speece, 2005).

Always keep in mind that screening instruments are imperfect; they catch many "false positives" in the "some risk" category. Nevertheless, they are helpful, especially when used knowledgably and in combination with other assessments. Critics of *DIBELS* and other screening measures should ask: "What's the alternative?"

- "To use lengthy assessments or teacher-made assessments that take a lot of time and that have little to no validation research behind them?"
- "To wait and see if students will 'get it' or not and then intervene once they are behind?"
- "To use 'authentic assessments' that may not assess component reading skills?"

From extensive experience, we are persuaded that the benefits of the most well-researched tools definitely outweigh the drawbacks.

Those benefits, however, depend on teachers' understanding of assessment and their ability to use data in problem-solving. Like all things in education, there are many ways that these assessments can be misused. The amount of professional development and coaching necessary for good use of data is considerable, according to one study completed in Florida (Roehrig, Duggar, Moats, Glover, & Mincey, 2008):

> ... In asking teachers to change their practices, it is unlikely we will have satisfactory results from professional development until the actual and perceived barriers to the use of progress-monitoring data are understood. Some of the most salient contextual variables, which teachers in this study described as barriers when attempting to use assessment data to inform instruction, included the following: (1) coach availability and quality of support received; (2) breakdown between receiving assessment results and what to do with children; (3) teacher knowledge; and (4) willingness of teachers to examine the effectiveness of their practices using student assessment results.

Thus, research confirms that the constructive use of screening data requires an investment in professional development. Teachers need time and good instruction themselves to understand how to administer and score each part of the screening instrument and how to interpret data. Further, they need sufficient coaching, mentoring, and support for a data-driven problem-solving model to work. The potential for misuse (or no use) is substantial unless these realities are addressed by administrative leadership.

DIBELS (6th Edition) and *DIBELS* Next

This module often refers to *DIBELS* because:

- this measure has been used the longest in research and practice;
- the data base for interpreting results is the largest;
- the measures are available in a print version, a free computer download version, reading program-embedded versions, and hand-held testing devices with direct links to a data bank; and
- there are *DIBELS* users in 48 of the 50 states (as of September 1, 2010).

In the revision called *DIBELS Next*, all of the *DIBELS* measures have been improved and two new measures have been added. These changes are found in *DIBELS Next*:

1. **New content.** All of the oral reading passages and forms are new.
2. **New and improved materials.** The new testing materials are organized to make *DIBELS* easier to administer and include reminder prompts integrated within the administration directions.
3. **New and improved directions.** All of the directions that are read to students and the reminder prompts have been revised and made more explicit to facilitate students' understanding of a task.
4. **Stratification.** A stratified random sampling procedure was used to improve the equivalence of the forms, and to more evenly distribute items of different difficulty. With stratified random sampling, items of similar difficulty appear in the same places on every form.
5. **Response patterns.** The measures include lists of common response patterns that the assessor can mark to help in planning instruction.

The two new measures are as follows:

1. **First Sound Fluency (FSF)**—Replaces Initial Sound Fluency (ISF). FSF is easier to administer and eliminates issues with ISF that were caused by ambiguity of some pictures, students guessing at answers, and starting and stopping the stopwatch for each item.
2. **Daze**—A new measure, based on maze procedures, has been added as an additional indicator of comprehension in grades 3–6. Daze can be administered in groups or individually.

Table 2.1 (next two pages) summarizes the changes made to the existing *DIBELS* (6th ed.) measures.

Table 2.1 Summary of Changes to Measures From *DIBELS* (6th ed.) to *DIBELS Next*

Measure	Description of Additional Changes
Letter Naming Fluency (LNF)	• All new forms. • New and improved materials with integrated reminders to enhance the administration of the measure. • New font that may be more familiar to younger students. • Stratification of test items to more evenly distribute the different letters across the form, and to improve the equivalence of the forms. • New, more explicit directions and reminders to facilitate students' understanding of the task. • A checklist of common response patterns to facilitate linkages to instruction.
Phoneme Segmentation Fluency (PSF)	• All new forms. • New and improved materials with integrated reminders to enhance the administration of the measure. • New layout to facilitate scoring. • No longer administered at the middle and end of first grade. • Stratification of test items based on four levels of segmentation difficulty. • New, more explicit directions and reminders to facilitate students' understanding of the task. • A checklist of common response patterns to facilitate linkages to instruction.
Nonsense Word Fluency (NWF)	• All new forms. • New and improved materials with integrated reminders to enhance the administration of the measure. • A new score, Whole Words Read (WWR), to replace Words Recoded Completely and Correctly (WRC). WWR measures the target skill of reading words as whole words. • New font that may be more familiar to younger students. • Stratification of test items in six difficulty/word-type categories, based on whether the word has two letters (VC) or three letters (CVC), and whether the consonants are more frequent or less frequent in English. • An even distribution of vowels, with each row of five items including one word with each vowel. • New, more explicit directions and reminders to facilitate students' understanding of the task and clarify that the preferred responses are whole words. Students are still permitted to provide individual letter sounds or to sound out the word while learning the skills. • A checklist of common response patterns to facilitate linkages to instruction.

Measure	Description of Additional Changes
DIBELS Oral Reading Fluency (DORF)	• All new passages developed using new procedures to ensure overall equivalent difficulty with *DIBELS* (6th ed.), but with a more consistent difficulty within each grade level. • New and improved materials with integrated reminders to enhance the administration of the measure. • New font that may be more familiar to younger students in first- and second-grade passages. • New, more explicit directions and reminders to facilitate students' understanding of the task. When administering three passages during benchmark assessment, shortened directions are now provided for the second and third passages. • A checklist of common response patterns to facilitate linkages to instruction.
Retell	• Retell is now included as a component of *DIBELS* Oral Reading Fluency (DORF) to indicate that the end-goal of reading is to read for meaning. • New and improved materials with integrated reminders to enhance the administration of the measure. • New, more explicit directions and reminders to facilitate students' understanding of the task. • A checklist of common response patterns to facilitate linkages to instruction.
Word Use Fluency-Revised (WUF-R)	• Available as an experimental measure while further research and development are conducted. Not routinely administered.

DIBELS Next Assessment by Grade Level

All *DIBELS* measures are timed.

- **Benchmark assessments** are given three times a year to all students in a grade. *Table 2.2* (next page) shows which indicators are administered in the fall, winter, and spring screenings.
- **Progress-monitoring assessments** are available in alternate forms for selected subtests, and are given to selected students as necessary.

Indicators are included at each grade level and at fall, winter, or spring assessments because of their ability to predict outcomes at that point in reading development. The "stepping stone" appearance of *Table 2.2* (next page) shows that the indicators that are useful in kindergarten and early grade 1 become less powerful or irrelevant predictors as children learn to read. As soon as students can read a passage, reading itself becomes the best predictor of later reading outcomes.

Table 2.2 *DIBELS Next* Measures, by Grade and Time of Year
NOTE: White blocks indicate when the measure is given.

	First Sound Fluency (FSF)	Nonsense Word Fluency (NWF)	Phoneme Segmentation Fluency (PSF)	Letter Naming Fluency (LNF)	Oral Reading Fluency (ORF) and Retell	Daze
K, Fall	✓		✓	✓		
K, Winter	✓		✓	✓		
K, Spring		✓	✓	✓		
K, PM		✓	✓	✓		
Grade 1						
1, Fall		✓	✓	✓		
1, Winter		✓		✓	✓	
1, Spring		✓		✓	✓	
1, PM		✓		✓	✓	
Grade 2						
2, Fall				✓	✓	
2, Winter					✓	
2, Spring					✓	
2, PM					✓	
Grade 3						
3, Fall					✓	✓
3, Winter					✓	✓
3, Spring					✓	✓
3, PM					✓	✓

PM = Progress-Monitoring

Exercise 2.2 | *DIBELS Next* and the Four-Part Processing Model

- As you review each of the six tasks included in the *DIBELS Next* assessment in this exercise, think carefully about the processing requirements of each one. Refer to the four-part processing model (*Figure 2.3*, below), supported by cognitive science (Adams, 1990; Rayner et al., 2001; Seidenberg & McClelland, 1989) and introduced in Module 1 of LETRS. In *Figure 2.3*, note what each indicator measures by placing its initials or name on the diagram. In addition, identify what skills on the hourglass figure (*Figure 2.4*, next page) the measure is targeting.

- If you are familiar with a different screening assessment (e.g., *TPRI, FAIR, AIMSweb, PALS*), determine which of the processing systems in *Figure 2.3* is most obviously measured by each task.

Figure 2.3   The Four-Part Processing Model for Word Recognition

(Rayner et al., 2001)

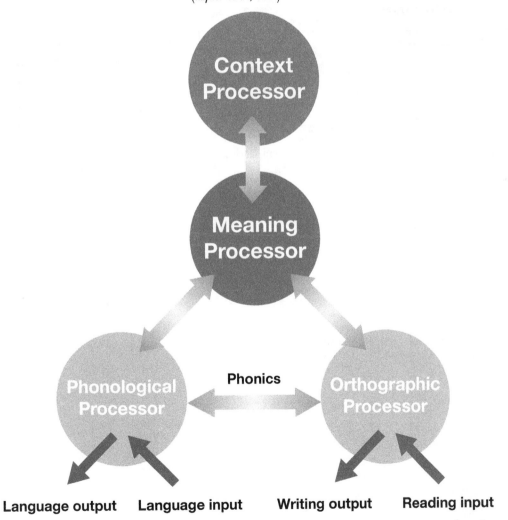

(continued)

Exercise 2.2 (continued)

Figure 2.4   The Hourglass Concept of Language Skill Progression
(Contributed by Carol Tolman, used with permission.)

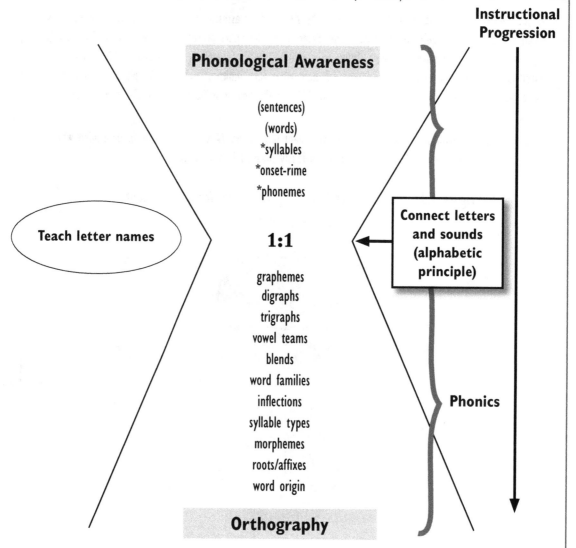

Instructional Progression

Phonological Awareness

(sentences)
(words)
*syllables
*onset-rime
*phonemes

Teach letter names

1:1

Connect letters and sounds (alphabetic principle)

graphemes
digraphs
trigraphs
vowel teams
blends
word families
inflections
syllable types
morphemes
roots/affixes
word origin

Phonics

Orthography

★ Phonology steps most supported by research to improve reading and spelling skills

Exercise 2.2 (continued)

- Each *DIBELS Next* indicator, what it measures, and an example of each are as follows:

1. **First Sound Fluency (FSF)** (*Beginning to mid-K*)
   This subtest measures a child's ability to identify, isolate, and pronounce the first sound of an orally presented word. The examiner says a word, and the child must isolate and pronounce the first sound. The score is based on the number of correct first sounds and partially correct responses given in 1 minute.

1 DIBELS® First Sound Fluency
Grade K/Benchmark 1

Test Items	Correct/2 points	Correct/1 point			Incorrect
1. laughed	/l/	/la/			0
2. pine	/p/	/pie/			0
3. skirt	/s/	/sk/	/sker/		0
4. flag	/f/	/fl/	/fla/		0
5. rang	/r/	/ra/			0
6. crow	/k/	/kr/			0
7. hide	/h/	/hie/			0
8. blame	/b/	/bl/	/blai/		0
9. deck	/d/	/de/			0
10. crab	/k/	/kr/	/kra/		0
11. bright	/b/	/br/	/brie/		0
12. knock	/n/	/no/			0
13. trash	/t/	/tr/	/tra/		0
14. list	/l/	/li/			0
15. spring	/s/	/sp/	/spr/	/spri/	0
16. chief	/ch/	/chea/			0
17. grand	/g/	/gr/	/gra/		0
18. sweat	/s/	/sw/	/swe/		0
19. shelf	/sh/	/she/			0
20. heard	/h/	/her/			0
21. crisp	/k/	/kr/	/kri/		0
22. plow	/p/	/pl/			0
23. hat	/h/	/ha/			0
24. sad	/s/	/sa/			0
25. swan	/s/	/sw/	/swo/		0
26. voice	/v/	/voy/			0
27. grapes	/g/	/gr/	/grai/		0
28. shell	/sh/	/she/			0
29. top	/t/	/to/			0
30. steal	/s/	/st/	/stea/		0

2-pt responses: _____

x 2: _____ + 1-pt responses: _____ = Total: _____

DIBELS® Next GK Benchmark Assessment Scoring Booklet / **3**

(continued)

Exercise 2.2 (continued)

2. **Letter Naming Fluency (LNF)** (*K to beginning Grade 1*)

Children are asked to name as many randomly mixed uppercase and lowercase letters as they can within 1 minute. The lowest 20 percent are at high risk for failing to achieve literacy benchmarks, whereas the group between the 20th and 40th percentiles is at some risk.

2 DIBELS® Letter Naming Fluency
Grade K/Benchmark 2

C	R	o	d	y	j	A	g	O	H
r	Y	G	N	x	f	a	D	Z	z
V	B	T	s	h	k	l	W	b	F
M	P	u	m	n	S	L	Q	e	c
U	q	K	p	E	t	J	i	w	X
I	v	F	X	U	m	w	H	h	s
g	L	D	i	N	d	T	S	r	B
Q	C	b	y	q	c	o	M	p	E
O	n	A	P	W	f	G	v	u	a
I	J	x	z	V	K	Y	l	e	t
k	Z	j	R	C	R	o	d	y	j

Total Correct: _____

LNF Response Patterns:

☐ Makes random errors   ☐ Doesn't track correctly

☐ Makes consistent errors on specific letter(s)   ☐ Other

☐ Says letter sound instead of letter name

Exercise 2.2 (continued)

3. **Phoneme Segmentation Fluency (PSF)** *(Mid-K to end Grade 1)*

The examiner gives the child a word or syllable with three or four phonemes and asks the child to say the individual sounds that make up the word (e.g., the examiner says, "**sat**," and the child says, "/s/ /ă/ /t/"). The score is the number of correct phonemes produced in 1 minute.

3 DIBELS® Phoneme Segmentation Fluency
Grade K/Benchmark 3

				Score
cave /k/ /ai/ /v/	take /t/ /ai/ /k/	holes /h/ /oa/ /l/ /z/	wake /w/ /ai/ /k/	/13
sides /s/ /ie/ /d/ /z/	hat /h/ /a/ /t/	world /w/ /er/ /l/ /d/	sick /s/ /i/ /k/	/14
match /m/ /a/ /ch/	told /t/ /oa/ /l/ /d/	wife /w/ /ie/ /f/	own /oa/ /n/	/12
clock /k/ /l/ /o/ /k/	bush /b/ /uu/ /sh/	goose /g/ /oo/ /s/	played /p/ /l/ /ai/ /d/	/14
will /w/ /i/ /l/	stopped /s/ /t/ /o/ /p/ /t/	bus /b/ /u/ /s/	look /l/ /uu/ /k/	/14
head /h/ /e/ /d/	shelf /sh/ /e/ /l/ /f/	like /l/ /ie/ /k/	near /n/ /i/ /r/	/13

Total: _____

PSF Response Patterns:

☐ Repeats word

☐ Makes random errors

☐ Says initial sound only

☐ Says onset rime

☐ Does not segment blends

☐ Adds sounds

☐ Makes consistent errors on specific sound(s)

☐ Other

(continued)

Exercise 2.2 (continued)

4. **Nonsense Word Fluency (NWF)** *(Mid-K—beginning Grade 2)*
   The child reads randomly ordered CVC words (e.g., **kib, pom, ruv**). All the vowels in the syllables are short vowels. The child receives credit for pronouncing individual sounds and extra credit for reading a whole syllable as a unit.

---

2 DIBELS® Nonsense Word Fluency
Grade 1/Benchmark 2

					CLS	WWR
▶ s a b	h e j	u t	z o s	n i n	/14 (14)	
b a v	n o l	v e m	i v	l u p	/14 (28)	
v i z	l e k	z a f	h o k	h u v	/15 (43)	
o c	n a j	w i d	r e s	m u p	/14 (57)	
u k	w i p	l a l	m o s	k e v	/14 (71)	
l o s	v i j	m u s	p e j	y a s	/15 (86)	
f o p	u j	v e s	b i j	t a l	/14 (100)	
k i b	m a v	y o c	k u f	e n	/14 (114)	
m e d	l i j	v a v	b o t	v u b	/15 (129)	
y u b	i g	s a j	k o f	t e p	/14 (143)	

Total correct letter sounds (CLS): _____

Total whole words read (WWR): _____

NWF Response Patterns:

☐ Says correct sounds out of order (sound-by-sound)

☐ Makes random errors

☐ Says correct sounds, does not recode

☐ Says correct sounds, recodes out of order

☐ Says correct sounds, recodes with incorrect sound(s)

☐ Says correct sounds and correctly recodes

☐ Doesn't track correctly

☐ Tries to turn nonsense words into real words

☐ Makes consistent errors on specific letter sound(s)

☐ Other

Exercise 2.2 (continued)

5. **Oral Reading Fluency (DORF)** with Retell (*Mid-Grade 1 to Grade 6*)
Benchmark passages at each grade level are used to measure accuracy and speed in oral reading of graded passages. Students are also asked to retell what they read. The measure is used to identify students in need of additional assessment and intervention and to monitor reading progress. Passages are calibrated by grade level and equated on each level. Students read each of three passages aloud for 1 minute. The student's score is the median (middle) words correct per minute (WCPM) score from the three passages. Errors are words omitted or substituted, or hesitations of more than 3 seconds. Immediate self-corrections are scored as accurate.

1 DIBELS® Oral Reading Fluency
Grade 2/Benchmark 1.3

Total words: _____

Errors (include skipped words): – _____

Words correct: = _____

The South Pole

0	What do you think of when you hear the words South Pole? Do you	14
14	see a pole in your mind? There really is a pole at the South Pole. It is	31
31	red and white like a candy cane. The flags of many countries surround	44
44	it. Scientists from these countries come to the South Pole. They work	56
56	together to study the climate.	61
61	The scientists have learned that the South Pole is the coldest place	73
73	on Earth. Even in the summer the temperature is below zero degrees.	85
85	It is so cold that most scientists only live at the South Pole during the	100
100	warmer summer months. Very few stay for the harsh winters. No one	112
112	else lives at the South Pole.	118
118	While the scientists are at the South Pole, they see some animals,	130
130	including penguins and seals. There are many fish in the water, too. In	143
143	the summer, some whales come to the South Pole. Even the whales	155
155	leave in the winter. It is just too cold.	164
164	Most people are surprised to learn that the South Pole is a dry	177
177	place. Yes, there is a lot of snow and ice, but little new sleet or snow falls	194
194	each year. The South Pole is like a frozen desert.	204
204	Perhaps you would like to see the South Pole for yourself. If you travel	218
218	there, you will see a few buildings where the scientists work and live. Of	232
232	course, you will see the red and white pole, too. Other than that, when	246
246	you look around, you will only see flat land covered with snow and ice.	260

8 / *DIBELS® Next G2 Benchmark Assessment Scoring Booklet*

(continued)

Exercise 2.2 (continued)

1 DIBELS® Oral Reading Fluency
Grade 2/Benchmark 1.3

The South Pole (continued)

Retell:

0	1	2	3	4	5	6	7	8	9	10	11	12	13	14	15	16	17	18	19	20	21	22	23	24	25
26	27	28	29	30	31	32	33	34	35	36	37	38	39	40	41	42	43	44	45	46	47	48			
49	50	51	52	53	54	55	56	57	58	59	60	61	62	63	64	65	66	67	68	69	70	71			
72	73	74	75	76	77	78	79	80	81	82	83	84	85	86	87	88	89	90	91	92	93	94			

Retell Total: _____

Quality of Response:
(Note: If the student provides only a main idea, it is considered one detail.)

1 Provides 2 or fewer details

2 Provides 3 or more details

3 Provides 3 or more details in a meaningful sequence

4 Provides 3 or more details in a meaningful sequence that captures a main idea

DIBELS® Next G2 Benchmark Assessment Scoring Booklet / **9**

Knowing that they will need to retell the passage keeps students from thinking that oral reading fluency is simply for reading fast. The DORF score itself correlates very highly with comprehension, but the retelling adds authenticity to the assessment. Retelling correlates about .59 with the DORF score itself, indicating that it is a good additional check on students' attention to meaning.

Exercise 2.2 (continued)

6. **Word Use Fluency (WUF)** (Experimental, Optional Task)

   WUF is designed to assess vocabulary knowledge and expressive language for students at each grade level. The examiner says a word and asks the student to use the word in a sentence. The score is the number of words the student can use correctly in a phrase, sentence, or expression within 1 minute.

   WUF is still an experimental and imperfect subtest, and the designers are not quite sure what the data show. When students are weak in this area relative to their decoding, and also are low on their Retell score, they may have a specific problem with vocabulary and expressive language.

   No benchmark goals are provided for WUF because more data need to be gathered to establish its relationship with other measures of literacy. A general rule is that students who score below the 20th percentile are at risk for poor reading outcomes, and those between the 20th and 40th percentile are at some risk.

- Taken together, the *DIBELS Next* indicators sample all of the key processing systems that support early reading acquisition.

Measures Used in Other Screening Assessments

The *AIMSweb* screening and progress-monitoring system is similar to *DIBELS* and is based on *DIBELS*, but it includes several different subtests. It measures the same skills, but it has added a few other indicators. In addition to Phoneme Segmentation Fluency (PSF), a measure of letter-sound association is used. The student is asked to say the sounds that letters or letter combinations represent.

The *Texas Primary Reading Inventory* (*TPRI*) includes a measure of reading real words in lists. The Virginia *PALS* test also uses graded word-list reading as a first "entry level" indicator of a student's overall reading skill. Graded word lists on *TPRI* are read for both speed and accuracy. Real-word reading is usually found to correlate as well, or better, with overall reading proficiency as nonsense-word reading. Both real- and nonsense-word reading depend on accuracy and fluency of decoding.

Spelling accuracy is included in *AIMSweb*, *TPRI*, and Virginia's *PALS*. However, only the *PALS* assessment provides guidance about the interpretation of spelling errors and links to instruction.

To supplement ORF results or to provide a second measure of reading comprehension, Maze Passages (in *AIMSweb*) or *DIBELS* Daze can be used from third grade on. This approach to assessing comprehension was developed and validated by Deno et al. (2001) and has been shown to be a satisfactory alternative to ORF as an estimate of overall reading proficiency. Correlations between Maze passages and ORF are very high; both are good measures of comprehension. In a Maze passage, words are omitted, and the student must select one of three possible replacement words to restore the meaning of the text. The number of correct replacements found in 2–3 minutes of reading (timing varies on different measures) is the index for comprehension. The following is an example of a third-grade level *DIBELS Next* Daze passage.

50   Chapter 2

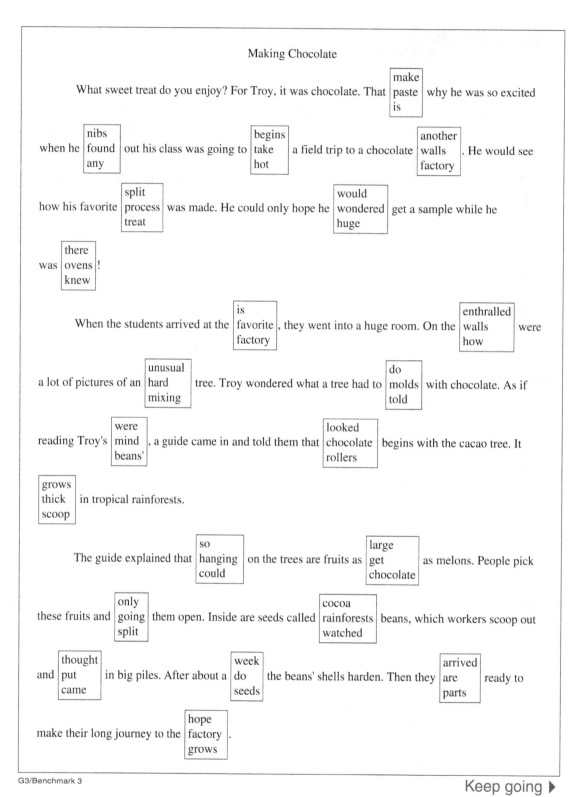

LETRS® Module 8, 2nd Edition

Troy saw that first the beans [harden / went / were] roasted in very hot ovens. The [reading / now / ovens] didn't look like any Troy

had [ever / outer / mind] seen, but the roasting beans smelled [seen / trip / great] ! Next, the beans went into another [next / machine / students]

that took off the hard outer [machines / treat / shells] and left the inside parts, called [are / nibs / roasted] . The guide explained

that the nibs [trees / room / are] the parts that go into the [roasting / chocolate / guide] . Troy watched as the nibs went into [big / yet / tour]

another machine. This machine crushed the [nibs / cooled / hanging] into a liquid. Troy was enthralled by the [excited / dark / lot]

liquid pouring out of the machine.

In the [next / large / last] part of the factory, Troy and the [sweet / might / other] students watched as the liquid went into

what [looked / passed / factory] like a very large mixing bowl. The [liquid / put / packaging] chocolate got mixed with dry milk and

[dark / sugar / take] to make a thick chocolate paste. The [when / thick / samples] chocolate passed through huge rollers. The

[better / melons / guide] told them that this part of the [moved / process / each] could take up to a week!

The [pictures / sugar / class] then moved on to see the [pick / already / then] mixed chocolate get poured into molds

[why / open / where] it cooled and hardened. The last [step / finally / field] was packaging. The students watched as [crushed / enjoy / machines]

Keep going ▶

LETRS® Module 8, 2nd Edition

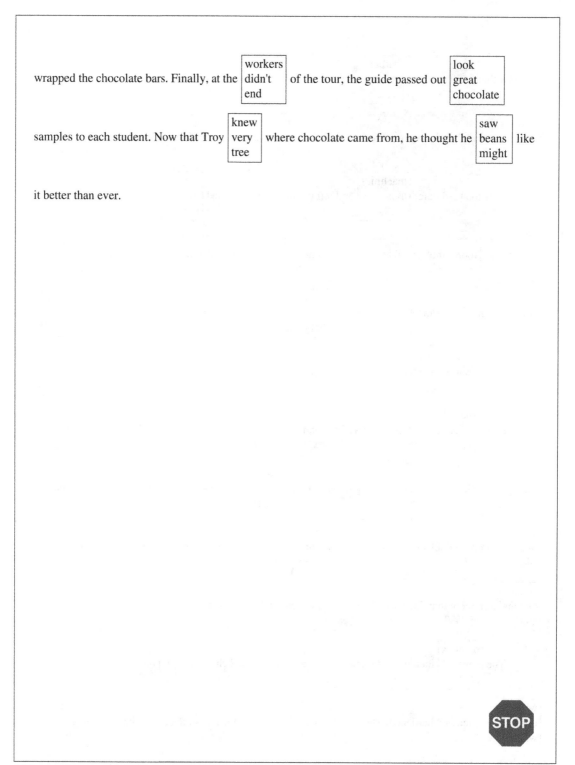

wrapped the chocolate bars. Finally, at the | workers / didn't / end | of the tour, the guide passed out | look / great / chocolate |

samples to each student. Now that Troy | knew / very / tree | where chocolate came from, he thought he | saw / beans / might | like

it better than ever.

STOP

Interpreting *DIBELS* Results

What Are the Benchmark Expectations for Children's Progress?

Benchmark goals and timelines for achieving them are summarized in *Table 2.3*. These revised benchmarks have been established by research involving 3,800 students in a nationally distributed sample. The benchmarks represent minimal levels of satisfactory progress for the lowest achieving students (Good, Gruba, & Kaminski, 2001). One hundred percent of students in the grade should achieve the benchmarks if 100 percent of the students are to read at grade level or better. The benchmarks from grade to grade follow a progression in reading development, wherein each step a student attains builds upon prior steps and is necessary for success in subsequent steps.

Table 2.3 *DIBELS Next* Benchmarks

Kindergarten

	Beginning of Year		Middle of Year		End of Year	
	Performance	Status	Performance	Status	Performance	Status
First Sound Fluency (FSF)	0–4	Intensive Support	0–19	Intensive Support	Not administered	
	5–9	Strategic Support	20–29	Strategic Support		
	10+	Core Support	30+	Core Support		
Letter Naming Fluency (LNF)	0–1	At risk	0–14	At risk	0–28	At risk
	2–7	Some risk	15–26	Some risk	29–39	Some risk
	8+	Low risk	27+	Low risk	40+	Low risk
Phoneme Segmentation Fluency (PSF)	Not administered		0–9	Intensive Support	0–24	Intensive Support
			10–19	Strategic Support	25–39	Strategic Support
			20+	Core Support	40+	Core Support
Nonsense Word Fluency (NWF)	Not administered		0–7	Intensive Support	0–14	Intensive Support
			8–16	Strategic Support	15–27	Strategic Support
			17+	Core Support	28+	Core Support

(continued)

First Grade

	Beginning of Year		Middle of Year		End of Year	
	Performance	**Status**	**Performance**	**Status**	**Performance**	**Status**
Letter Naming Fluency (LNF)	0–24	At risk	Not administered during this period.		Not administered during this period.	
	25–36	Some risk				
	37+	Low risk				
Phoneme Segmentation Fluency (PSF)	0–24	Intensive Support	Not administered during this period.		Not administered during this period.	
	25–39	Strategic Support				
	40+	Core Support				
Nonsense Word Fluency-Correct Letter Sounds (NWF-CLS)	0–17	Intensive	0–32	Intensive	0–46	Intensive
	18–26	Strategic	33–42	Strategic	47–57	Strategic
	27+	Core	43+	Core	58+	Core
NWF-Whole Words Read (NWF-WWR)		Intensive	0–2	Intensive	0–5	Intensive
	0	Strategic	3–7	Strategic	6–12	Strategic
	1–50	Core	8–50	Core	13–50	Core
Oral Reading Fluency-Words Correct Per Minute (ORF-WCPM)	Not administered during this period.		0–15	Intensive	0–31	Intensive
			16–22	Strategic	32–46	Strategic
			23+	Core	47+	Core
ORF-Accuracy	Not administered		0–67%	Intensive	0–81%	Intensive
			68%–77%	Strategic	82%–89%	Strategic
			78%–100%	Core	90%–100%	Core
ORF-Retell	Not administered				0–14	Strategic
					15–94	Core

Second Grade

	Beginning of Year		Middle of Year		End of Year	
	Performance	Status	Performance	Status	Performance	Status
Nonsense Word Fluency-Correct Letter Sounds (NWF-CLS)	0–34	Intensive	Not administered during this period.		Not administered during this period.	
	35–53	Strategic				
	54+	Core				
NWF-Whole Words Read (NWF-WWR)	0–5	Intensive	NA		NA	
	6–12	Strategic				
	13–50	Core				
Oral Reading Fluency-Whole Words Read (ORF-WWR)	0–36	Intensive	0–54	Intensive	0–64	Intensive
	37–51	Strategic	55–71	Strategic	65–86	Strategic
	52+	Core	72+	Core	87+	Core
ORF-Accuracy	0–80%	Intensive	0–90%	Intensive	0–92%	Intensive
	81%–89%	Strategic	91%–95%	Strategic	93%–96%	Strategic
	90%–100%	Core	96%–100%	Core	97%–100%	Core
ORF-Retell Quality	NA		0	Intensive	0	Intensive
			1	Strategic	1	Strategic
			2–4	Core	2–4	Core

Third Grade

	Beginning of Year		Middle of Year		End of Year	
	Performance	Status	Performance	Status	Performance	Status
Oral Reading Fluency-Whole Words Read (ORF-WWR)	0–54	Intensive	0–67	Intensive	0–79	Intensive
	55–69	Strategic	68–85	Strategic	80–99	Strategic
	70+	Core	86+	Core	100+	Core
ORF-Accuracy	0–88%	Intensive	0–91%	Intensive	0–93%	Intensive
	89%–94%	Strategic	92%–95%	Strategic	94%–96%	Strategic
	95%–100%	Core	96%–100%	Core	97%–100%	Core
ORF-Retell	0–9	Intensive	0–17	Intensive	0–19	Intensive
	10–19	Strategic	18–25	Strategic	20–29	Strategic
	20–94	Core	26–94	Core	30–94	Core
ORF-Retell Quality		Intensive		Intensive	1	Intensive
	1	Strategic	1	Strategic	2	Strategic
	2–4	Core	2–4	Core	3–4	Core
Daze Adjusted Score	0–4	Intensive	0–6	Intensive	0–13	Intensive
	5–7	Strategic	7–10	Strategic	14–18	Strategic
	8–51	Core	11–51	Core	19–51	Core

Are a Child's Assessment Scores Representative of His "True" Abilities?

Screening measures, like all assessments of human abilities, contain measurement error. An obtained score may not be representative of what the student seems to do in the classroom. This can and does happen for a variety of reasons: examiners make mistakes; young students may be insecure, inattentive, or unfamiliar with the requirements of the task, or they just may be having a bad day.

The advantage of *DIBELS* or similar measures is that students can be easily rechecked if their estimate of risk appears to be misjudged or the scores do not agree with one another or with teacher observations. The progress-monitoring booklets provide alternate testing forms that can be used to retest a student. By retesting on a different day or with a different examiner, we can be more confident that the scores are reliable. Two or three retests are usually enough to get a consistent picture of the student's actual level of skill. In addition, other assessments of the same skills can be employed to verify findings.

The first step: Grouping students by risk level

In *Exercise 2.3*, we will look closely at some *DIBELS* results for a kindergarten and a grade 1 classroom. As you look closely at these data, you will notice that scores are "weighted" within a prediction formula—rather than simply added up—in order to obtain the instructional recommendation. Each score is followed by a letter code:

- **C** = "in need of core instructional support" or at the benchmark level.
- **S** = "in need of strategic intervention" or somewhat below benchmark and mildly at risk.
- **I** = "in need of intensive intervention" or significantly at risk and with a low chance of performing on grade-level in reading.

Exercise 2.3 | Interpret *DIBELS* Screening Data for K and First Grade

- Class reports for three grades in the same school are provided in this exercise. Each grade level is preceded by specific questions you can answer after looking closely at the *DIBELS* data. (Your presenter may provide you with student data sets on cards that can be manipulated as you sort through and compare students' results.)

Kindergarten Class Data, End of Year

1. What is the "risk" cut-point for letter naming fluency (LNF)? How many students are at risk? At some risk? _____

_____

2. What does letter naming predict? _____

_____

3. How many students are at benchmark levels in PSF? Below benchmark?_____

_____

4. What does PSF measure? How is PSF related to NWF? _____

_____

5. How many students are at benchmark levels in NWF? Below benchmark? _____

_____

6. What does NWF measure? How is NWF related to real-word reading and oral-reading fluency?_____

_____

7. Many of these students are off to a poor start in basic reading skills. Before you discuss intervention groups, identify the components of instruction that should be strengthened in this classroom's core (Tier 1) reading program. _____

_____

_____

8. Sort the students by their risk level on each measure. What are some possible groupings for small-group intervention? _____

_____

(continued)

Exercise 2.3 (continued)

Kindergarten *DIBELS* Data

Student	Letter Naming Fluency (LNF)	Phoneme Segmentation Fluency (PSF)	Nonsense Word Fluency (Correct Letter Sounds) (NWF-CLS)	Composite Score and Instructional Level*
Keith	5 (AR) Doesn't know (DK) uppercase or lowercase	28 (S) Incomplete segmentation	0 (I) No letter-sound knowledge	33 = Intensive
Mary	11 (AR) Many errors; DK b, p, u, q, e, l	27 (I) Sound combinations, incomplete segmentation	2 (I) Almost no letter-sound knowledge	40 = Intensive
Misty	12 (AR) DK g, b, f, e, v, k, j	1 (I) Confused by task, could not do training item	0 (I) Could not do training item.	13 = Intensive
Kara	12 (AR) DK g, u, b, w, f, v, e, k, y	31 (S) Incomplete segmentation	6 (I) Limited letter-sound knowledge	49 = Intensive
Nate	20 (AR) Limited letter knowledge	31 (S) Says onset-rime	4 (I) Very limited letter-sound knowledge	55 = Intensive
Shawn	23 (AR) DK u, p, w, q, y, d	11 (I) No vowel sounds	3 (I)	37 = Intensive
Caitlin	24 (AR) DK y, p, w, q	22 (I) Incomplete segmentation	6 (I) Says /ŭ/ for most vowels	52 = Intensive
Nicholas	24 (AR) DK b, p, q, k, d, h	29 (S) Incomplete segmentation	4 (I) Wanted to give letter names, not sounds	57 = Intensive
Cody	27 (AR) DK some letters	31 (S) Some words completely segmented	11 (I) DK vowel sounds	69 = Intensive

Exercise 2.3 (continued)

Kindergarten *DIBELS* Data

Student	Letter Naming Fluency (LNF)	Phoneme Segmentation Fluency (PSF)	Nonsense Word Fluency (Correct Letter Sounds) (NWF-CLS)	Composite Score and Instructional Level*
Tim	**28** (AR) DK p, b, d, q	**18** (I) Some single phonemes, some word parts	**13** (I) Knows short i and short e only	**59** = Intensive
Rolf	**29** (AR) Accurate names	**27** (S) Some single phonemes, some onset-rime	**21** (S) DK short a	**77** = Intensive
Michael	**31** (SR) DK h	**29** (S) Single phonemes but incomplete	**11** (I) DK short o or short u	**71** = Intensive
Jeri	**31** (SR) DK u, b, l, d, z, h	**16** (I) Says initial sound only	**9** (I) DK short i, u, o	**56** = Intensive
Jocelyn	**33** (SR) b/d confusion	**31** (S) Some single phonemes, some phoneme groups	**19** (S) b/d confusion	**83** = Intensive
Craig	**33** (SR) b/d/q confusion	**7** (I) Mostly says whole words	**9** (I) DK vowels	**49** = Intensive
Robert	**34** (SR) b/d/p confusion, u/n confusion	**6** (I) Trouble segmenting even the first sound	**11** (I) DK vowels	**51** = Intensive
Kelly	**38** (SR) b/d confusion	**57** (C) Segments individual phonemes	**12** (I) DK vowels, b/d confusion	**107** = Strategic
Mick	**40** (LR) b/d confusion	**32** (S) Some individual sounds, some larger units	**19** (S) DK short vowels i, u, o	**91** = Strategic

(continued)

Exercise 2.3 (continued)

Kindergarten *DIBELS* Data

Student	Letter Naming Fluency (LNF)	Phoneme Segmentation Fluency (PSF)	Nonsense Word Fluency (Correct Letter Sounds) (NWF-CLS)	Composite Score and Instructional Level*
Ray	**41** (LR) b/d confusion, v/y, DK h	**5** (I) Confused letter names and sounds; couldn't do training item	**10** (I) b/d, short vowels, n/h	**56 = Intensive**
Len	**43** (LR) Unsure of b/d/g	**42** (C) Segments individual sounds, not blends	**11** (I) DK short vowels	**96 = Strategic**
Omar	**45** (LR) Totally accurate	**47** (C) Segments phonemes; trouble with blends	**23** (S) b/d confusion, DK short u, short e	**115 = Strategic**
Sally	**54** (LR) b/d confusion	**29** (S) Some individual sounds, some partially segmented	**18** (S) DK vowels	**101 = Strategic**

*The composite score for kindergarten benchmark goals is computed by adding FSF, PSF, and NWF-CLS. To be at or above benchmark, the composite must be 119 or better. To be in the strategic range, the score must be 89–118. Below 89 is the range of intensive instructional support.

Exercise 2.3 (continued)

First-Grade Class Data, End of Year

1. How many students are below benchmark in NWF-CLS? What does this result suggest about the classroom (Tier 1) instruction? _____

   _____

2. Do the NWF-CLS or NWF-WWR scores tell you which phonics skills the students need to learn and practice? _____

   _____

3. Who is below benchmark in DORF-WC? _____

   _____

4. Who meets benchmark on NWF-CLS but is below benchmark in DORF-WC? What other information do you need to interpret this result, and what might it mean? _____

   _____

   _____

5. Who is relatively better at oral reading than at NWF-CLS? Should the teacher(s) do anything specific to help those students? _____

   _____

   _____

6. Who looks as if he/she might be at benchmark in DORF-WC but weak in comprehension? What factors may play a role in these results? _____

   _____

7. Who should be recommended for strategic intervention (small groups, 3–5 times/week)? What is your initial thought about an instructional approach (or approaches) that might accelerate the growth of these students? _____

   _____

   _____

8. Who may have a learning disability or other handicapping condition? In general terms, what kind of instruction would you recommend for this student? _____

   _____

(continued)

Exercise 2.3 (continued)

First-Grade *DIBELS* Data

Student	NWF-CLS	NWF-WWR	DORF-WC	DORF-Accuracy	Retell	Composite*
Bob	142 (C)	49 (C)	164 (C) Speed reads but does comprehend	99%	32 (C)	367 (C)
Hannah	62 (C)	23 (C)	153 Limited comprehension; doesn't recall	99%	19 (C)	304 (C)
Amy	141 (C)	48 (C)	121 (C)	100%	45 (C)	322 (C)
Evan	89 (C)	27 (C)	87 (C)	98%	54 (C)	240 (C)
Luther	81 (C)	25 (C)	95 (C) Skips words, doesn't self-correct errors	97%	35 (C)	244 (C)
Tonya	79 (C)	25 (C)	94 (C)	98%	37 (C)	243 (C)
Linda	107 (C)	37 (C)	88 (C) Self-corrects, reads attentively	100%	33 (C)	267 (C)
Mark	66 (C)	22 (C)	73 (C) Self-corrects, reads carefully	100%	42 (C)	222 (C)
Eileen	51 (C)	15 (C)	40 (C) Reads well; self-corrects, decodes	100%	34 (C)	204 (C)
Payton	81 (C)	24 (C)	72 (C)	94%	26 (C)	207 (C)
Chloe	33 (I)	11 (S)	60 (C) Limited comprehension; anxious; omits words	97%	9 (C)	181 (C)

Exercise 2.3 (continued)

First-Grade *DIBELS* Data

Student	NWF-CLS	NWF-WWR	DORF-WC	DORF-Accuracy	Retell	Composite*
Zach	**73** (C)	**24** (C)	**59** (C)	95%	**25** (C)	**200 (C)**
Forrest	**45** (I) Substitutes long for short vowels	**9** (S)	**56** (C) Errors violate passage meaning	90%	**21** (C) Weak retell	**149 (S)**
Art	**34** (I) Substitutes long for short vowels	**9** (S)	**56** (C) Tries to apply decoding strategy	97%	**27** (C) Weak retell	**173 (C)**
Grace	**74** (C)	**24** (C)	**46** (S) Self-corrects, reads accurately	96%	**36** (C) Retell quality very good	**187 (C)**
Olivia	**68** (C)	**12** (S)	**42** (S) Errors violate passage meaning	89%	**43** (C) Retell good for what she reads	**141 (S)**
Garrett	**67** (C)	**20** (C)	**26** (I) Many word recognition errors	76%	**14** (S) Retell good for what he reads	**99 (S)**
Nat	**49** (S) b/d confusion, insecure on short vowels	**11** (S)	**28** (I) Struggles to read words	85%	**20** (C)	**113 (S)**
Thomas	**25** (I)	**0** (I)	**(9)**	9 Discontinued	NA	**(I)**

*Composite at the end of grade 1 is calculated by adding (NWF-WWR x 2) + (DORF-WC) + (Accuracy Value from Conversion Table). The composite score must be 155 or above to be at benchmark (in need of core support). The composite score strategic range is 111–154, and the intensive range is 110 or below.

Exercise 2.4 | What Can and Can't Be Learned From Screening

- Look over the decision-making flow charts (*Figures 1.11* and *1.12*) at the end of Chapter 1.
- With a small group, list and then summarize what can be learned from a valid screening measure. Also think about what cannot be learned from screening, or what else you would need to know to address a student's reading problem with an approach that makes sense.

1. What can be learned from screening:

_____

_____

_____

2. What cannot be learned from screening:

_____

_____

_____

_____

_____

_____

_____

_____

Summary

In Chapter 1, we presented a strategy for student assessment that calls for the use of universal screening three times per year in kindergarten and first grade, and optional screening for all students who are consistently well above grade level in grades 2 and 3. In Chapter 2, we reviewed screening measures in more depth, with a focus on *DIBELS Next* as an example of a valid and reliable screening tool. After looking at class data, we also considered what can and cannot be learned from using a valid and well-researched screening process.

That being said, we are only at first base! We have answered the question, "Who needs help?"—who is at greatest risk of reading failure—but we have not answered the questions:

- What kind of help do they need?
- Why do they need the help?
- Is the help helping?
- If not, what needs to be changed?

The next step in assessment requires us to:

- look closely at the data we have;
- decide what additional diagnostic data we need; and
- make educated guesses about instruction to be delivered.

Chapter 3

What Kind of Help Is Needed?

The Subtypes of Reading Difficulty

Learner Objectives for Chapter 3

- Identify the major subgroups of students with reading difficulty.
- Know why and for whom diagnostic surveys of phonics, spelling, and phonological processing are useful.
- Become familiar with a decoding survey and spelling survey.
- Practice error analysis.
- Understand the limitations of standardized comprehension assessments.
- Prepare to use observation, qualitative, and quantitative testing to evaluate comprehension.
- Use a developmental framework and knowledge of subtypes to judge what kind of help students need.

Warm-Up: Validated Reading Subtypes

- Using the subtype list below (and with reference to Module 1 of LETRS), identify inside the diagram circles the three validated subtypes of students with reading difficulties—mild to severe—in scientific research studies (e.g., Fletcher et al., 2007; Hulme & Snowling, 2009; Tunmer, 2008). (Subtypes of poor readers often overlap, as the Venn diagram suggests.)
    - Auditory perception
    - Orthographic processing speed/fluency
    - Low IQ
    - Sensory-motor skills
    - Kinesthesis ("hands–on" learners)
    - Vocabulary
    - Phonological processing
    - Visual perception
    - Oral/written language comprehension
    - Short-term memory

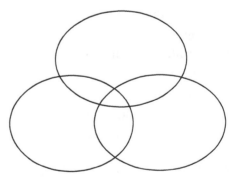

Not All Reading Problems Are Alike

Subcomponents of Reading

Genetic, environmental, and instructional factors all contribute to the growth of reading skill. All these factors together influence the development of cognition and oral and written language. In previous LETRS modules, we represented the causal factors—genetic, environmental, and instructional—with several theoretical models, including the four-part processing model of word recognition and Scarborough's (2001) "reading rope." Recall that the two main areas into which the strands of the rope are organized are *language comprehension and word recognition* (see *Figure 1.4* on page 13 in Chapter 1).

Because the subskills that underlie successful reading are fairly well understood by researchers at this point (Berninger & Wolf, 2009; Fletcher et al., 2007; Joshi, 2005; Pennington, 2009; Wolf & Katzir-Cohen, 2001), studies have been able to address questions such as:

- What components are most important at certain points in reading development?
- How many students are likely to have problems with specific components?
- How distinct are those subgroups?
- Do those subgroups respond differently to instruction?
- If so, what kind of instruction works best for what subgroup?

Extensive and convergent research generally finds that there are three distinct subgroups of students with reading problems:

1. Those with significant weaknesses in phonological processing and word-reading skills that depend on phonological processing;
2. Those with slow or dysfluent printed word recognition, most likely related to a specific problem with orthographic processing; and
3. Those with oral and written language comprehension.

Each subgroup has been shown to be somewhat independent of the others. The fact that subgroups exist reflects back to the structure and function of the reading brain, sketched in LETRS Module 1. Several processing systems in several brain regions are recruited to support reading, and the brain must build a "reading machine" out of networks that were not originally designed for reading (Dehaene, 2009). Because several distinct neural networks are recruited to enable reading, it is logical (and factual) that disruptions in one or more of those networks can cause reading difficulties. The existence of major subtypes with varying symptoms supports an important reality: *The emphasis of instruction should vary according to the nature of a student's problem.* No one program or intervention will be appropriate for all students who are "below benchmark."

Phonological processing weakness

Problems with word recognition that originate with a weakness in phonological processing are by far the most common kind of reading difficulty in the early grades. About 70–80 percent of poor readers (conservatively, according to some researchers) have trouble with accurate and fluent word recognition, and this problem in turn originates with weaknesses in phonological processing. The term *dyslexia* is appropriate for a reading and spelling problem that originates with a phonological processing and word recognition difficulty and that persists in spite of adequate instruction. These poor readers have obvious trouble learning sound-symbol correspondences, sounding out and blending words, and spelling.

Slow processing speed

Another 10–15 percent of poor readers appear to be accurate, but too slow, in word recognition and text reading. They have specific weaknesses with *speed* of word recognition and automatic recall of word spellings, although they do relatively well on tests of phoneme awareness and other phonological skills. They have trouble developing automatic recognition of words by sight and tend to spell phonetically, but not accurately. This subgroup is thought to have relative strengths in phonological processing, but the nature of their relative weakness is still debated by reading scientists (Fletcher et al., 2007; Katzir et al., 2006; Wolf & Bowers, 1999). Some argue that the problem is primarily one of timing or processing speed, and others propose that there is a specific deficit within the orthographic processor that affects the storage and recall of exact letter sequences (Stainthorp, Stuart, Powell, Quinlan, & Garwood, 2010). This processing speed/orthographic subgroup generally has milder difficulties with reading than students with phonological processing deficits.

Oral and written language comprehension

Yet another 10–15 percent of poor readers (excluding students learning English as a second language) in grades K–3 appear to decode words better than they can comprehend the meanings of passages. These poor readers are distinguished from dyslexic poor readers because they can read words accurately and quickly and they can spell. Their problems are caused by disorders of social reasoning, abstract verbal reasoning, or language comprehension. As students get older, especially around grade 5, the proportion who demonstrates poor comprehension relative to their decoding skills increases because the cognitive and language demands of text reading increase. Students with limited verbal comprehension will make less and less progress if their abstract verbal reasoning, vocabulary, background knowledge, and familiarity with literary genres are not sufficient to support advanced reading comprehension.

Combined factors

Most poor readers are affected by two or three of these core problems; the "pure" subtypes are less common than the mixed subtypes. When students have trouble processing the phonological features of words, they often have concomitant problems with oral and written language comprehension (Berninger & Wolf, 2009). Some or all aspects of language structure—speech sounds, morphemes, sentences, semantic relationships, and discourse organization—may be difficult for students to process.

Further, some weakness with processing speed and fluency is a feature of most reading and writing problems. Students who cannot decode accurately are often too slow on measures of oral reading fluency. Only a few students seem to have specific, circumscribed problems with symbol naming speed when phonological processing is strong and language is average or above.

If a student has a prominent and specific weakness in either phonological or rapid print (naming-speed) processing, he or she is said to have a *single deficit* in word recognition. If a student has a combination of phonological and naming-speed deficits that adversely affect word recognition, he or she is said to have a *double deficit* (Wolf, 2007; Wolf & Bowers, 1999). Double-deficit students are more common than single-deficit, and they are also the most challenging to teach. Related and coexisting problems in students with reading difficulties, especially dyslexia, often include:

- faulty pencil grip and letter formation;
- attention problems;
- anxiety;
- task avoidance;
- weak impulse control;
- distractibility;
- problems with comprehension of spoken language; and
- confusion of mathematical signs and computation processes.

About 30–40 percent of all students with attention deficit hyperactivity disorder (ADHD) also have a reading disorder (Aylward, 2007).

Environmental or neurobiological?

One reason for the current emphasis on RtI is that screening and diagnostic tests may be insufficient for determining the nature or origin of a reading or writing problem. Some children come to school without the kind of exposure to books, book language, and vocabulary that supports the development of literacy; they can be called "experience-deficient." Some students have generally weak verbal abilities and academic learning in all areas. An increasing number of students are learning English as a second language. Some students fall behind, even though they are capable of learning, simply because their instruction has been insufficient. And some have legitimate, biologically based learning disabilities that deserve to be properly assessed, classified, and treated through remedial and special education.

Other conditions that may impair reading and writing

This module is focused on assessment of reading and writing difficulties that are best treated through academic interventions. Nevertheless, in asking the questions, "Why does a student need help?" and "What kind of help?" it is important for school personnel to keep in mind the less frequent developmental disorders that may coexist with reading, spelling, or writing disabilities, and that may require other kinds of treatment (Pennington, 2009):

- **Intellectual Disability** (IQ below 70): Problems with adaptive behavior; low in all academic skills.
- **Language Impairment:** Poor grammar development, particularly past-tense acquisition; low verbal abilities, compared to non-verbal abilities; poor phonological skills, often with poor phonological memory.
- **Speech-Sound Disorder:** Delays and differences in articulation of speech sounds; often overlaps with language impairment; often, but not always, involves deficits in other phonological skills.

- **Developmental Coordination Disorder:** Substantial delays in motor skills such as balance and coordination; impairment of handwriting; often associated with visual-spatial deficits and slow processing speed.
- **Autism Spectrum Disorder:** Impairment of social cognition and social communication; stereotypical behavior and restricted patterns of interaction.
- **Attention Deficit Hyperactivity Disorder**, including inattentive subtype, hyperactive-impulsive subtype, and combined.

These conditions, although uncommon in the general population, may require multidisciplinary evaluations and diagnostic work-ups that go far beyond the academic assessment that is our focus here. If any of these conditions is suspected, child-study teams should not wait to undertake a comprehensive evaluation and an intervention plan. After all, if you were the child's parent, would you be satisfied to hear that your child is "Tier 2" or "Tier 3?" Wouldn't you want to know if medical treatment or other therapies were indicated?

Exercise 3.1	**Review the Subtypes of Reading Difficulty**

- In the space below, draw a diagram of the three major subtypes of reading difficulty. Label the major subtypes, show how they overlap, and list the characteristics of students in each group.

- To make this exercise more active, pretend that your class is a group of second-graders who all scored below benchmark on a screening test. Divide into subtypes and have each subtype describe and/or role-play their identifying characteristics.

Some Realities of Individual Differences— or Why Diagnostics Can Be Complicated

Word recognition problems—with either accuracy, speed, or both—characterize the majority of poor readers in the primary grades. While their instruction should include systematic and explicit phonics, it should also address oral and written language comprehension because decoding problems seldom exist in isolation. Sometimes, however, a student seems to have a "glitch" in a specific processing system. Occasionally a student will be good at comprehension and poor at decoding, with primary weaknesses in the phonological and/ or orthographic processors, or good at decoding and poor at comprehension, with primary weaknesses in the meaning and context processors.

Students who have word recognition problems may differ from each other. Some may be relatively accurate but too slow, and may lack sufficient speed to support comprehension. Their intervention plans can focus primarily on building fluency in word recognition and text-reading (see Module 5 of LETRS). Most students who are not meeting fluency benchmarks, however, need to improve the accuracy and fluency of word recognition. If students are less than 97 percent accurate in oral text reading, word study should be a strong focus of instruction, along with other components.

Some students read quickly but are inaccurate. They make many word recognition errors that erode their comprehension. These students may be impulsive and have trouble slowing down enough to look closely at the print, recall the sounds associated with the letters, and blend those sounds together. Instructional history may be the culprit in some of these cases. Students may be inaccurate at word reading because they have been encouraged to guess at words on the basis of context instead of: (a) looking carefully at the whole word; (b) using grapheme-phoneme correspondences to decode the word; and (c) checking the sense of what they are reading. Once established, these habits of contextual guessing are difficult to break, and students continue to be at a loss when faced with unfamiliar content words.

When students decode the words accurately but struggle to comprehend, a different approach to instruction is going to be necessary (Aaron et al., 2008; Tunmer & Greaney, 2010). Therefore, the goal of diagnostic assessment is to determine who needs a code-emphasis approach—with a focus on accuracy—and who needs something else, such as a strong focus on oral and written language comprehension. The decision-making flow charts, *Figures 1.10* and *1.11*, introduced in Chapter 1 and referenced on the next page, suggest road maps for selecting diagnostic assessments and deciding what to do with whom.

Figure 1.10 Decision-Making Model for Grades K–1

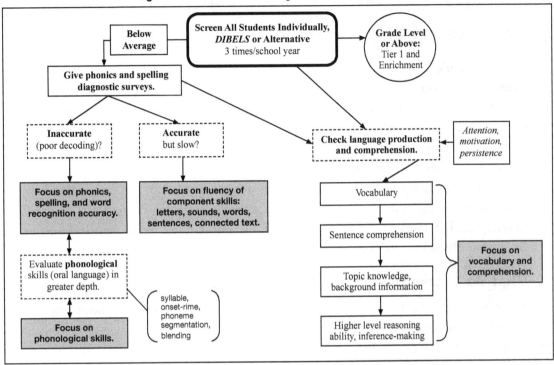

Figure 1.11 Decision-Making Model for Grades 2–3

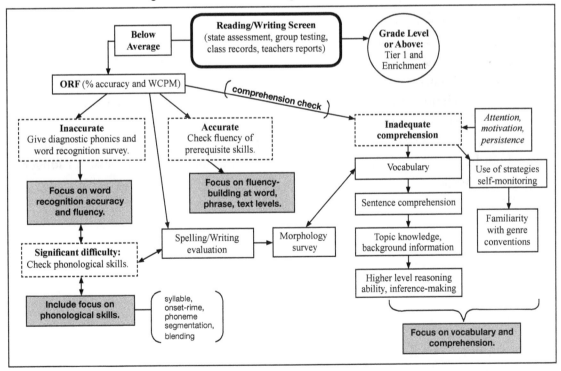

Strategy for Diagnostic Assessment of Basic Reading Skill

Diagnostic work is a process of gathering data, asking questions of that data, and forming hypotheses based on your knowledge of literacy, learning, the individual student, and instruction. The hypotheses lead to decisions about the content, design, and intensity of instruction for a student or group of students. Teachers then must work hard with students to implement the instruction or intervention. The diagnostic hypotheses are then evaluated with progress-monitoring data and observations.

The left-side branches of the flow charts in *Figures 1.10* and *1.11* are followed and explained through the rest of this chapter. The strategic approach represented in the flow charts is depicted in a series of key questions and the actions you might take to address them. A case study is threaded into the discussion, question by question.

1. What do I already know about the student?

Gather student data, including information from previous grades, school attendance, health history, and family history. Look at existing data regarding the student's overall reading proficiency levels. Did the student pass the state's outcome test? Is the student in the "at some risk" or "at risk" categories on screening?

Case Study: Background Information

The student in our featured case study had a long history of difficulty with letter naming and sound-symbol learning in kindergarten and first grade. He repeated first grade. On assessments of cognitive ability, he scored above average (about the 85th percentile) in oral language comprehension and verbal reasoning. He had been read to early and often by professional parents. His background and topic knowledge were very well developed, so that he could slowly muddle his way through passages even if he missed a lot of the words. While this approach enabled him to manage easier content, it did not help him when the topic was unfamiliar or when he had to decipher longer, unfamiliar words.

---

2. Is word recognition a weakness that should be evaluated in more depth?

Most of the time, the answer to this question will be "yes." If a student is below benchmark in oral reading or on other indicators, the next step is to determine if the student is weak in phonics and word-reading accuracy, fluency, or both, and to plan instruction accordingly.

To determine if additional assessment is necessary, examine the ORF and Retell transcript or comprehension screener. If the student is below benchmark on ORF, look at both words correct per minute (WCPM) and the accuracy rate. If the accuracy rate is less than 97 percent, or if you have observed the student making errors in word recognition and struggling with decoding, you definitely need to check the student's ability to read real words and nonsense words out of context and to associate phonemes with graphemes during decoding. If the ORF accuracy percentage is high and the student is also accurate on measures of phoneme segmentation and nonsense or real-word reading, but the reading rate is slow, it is likely that fluency-oriented instruction will fit the student's needs.

Case Study: Looking at an Oral Reading Transcript

Figure 3.1 (next page) shows an out-of-level ORF assessment given to our third-grade boy. He was tested out of level because of his history of moderately severe reading difficulties. At mid-third grade, the average third-grader reads at about 92 WCPM; our student read at a rate of 58 WCPM. In addition to reading slowly, this student made some decoding errors—or simply stopped in his tracks—when reading unfamiliar content words. Nevertheless, he did understand what he read (retell was good). Data from other assessments confirmed that this boy could employ his strong vocabulary, oral language, and background knowledge to facilitate reading comprehension and compensate somewhat for his struggles with decoding. Additional diagnostic assessment of his knowledge of phonics was indicated because of his weaknesses in basic reading skill.

Figure 3.1 ORF Recording, *DIBELS* 2.2 Benchmark, Third-Grade Student

Benchmark 2.2
DIBELS® Oral Reading Fluency

Keiko the Killer Whale

Keiko the whale was ~~captured~~ near Iceland and brought to	10
California. He became a famous performer who did tricks at a	21
theme park. He even ~~started~~ starred in a movie! Keiko is an Orca	33
whale. Orcas are called killer whales because they feed on seals.	44
Keiko was not ~~healthy~~ hearing at the theme park. He was thin and his	57
skin was covered with sores.] His body was too big for the tank	70
he lived in. The water was not cold enough for him to be	83
comfortable. He couldn't get enough exercise to be healthy. He	93
was not a happy whale.	98
Keiko was taken to the Oregon Coast Aquarium to get	108
healthy and eventually be released back into the wild. At the	119
aquarium, he ate the kind of fish he would have caught himself	131
in the ocean. He lived in a very large tank full of cool ocean	145
water. Trainers took care of him and helped him remember what	156
it was like to be wild again.	163
Keiko ate well and exercised every day. He gained about two	174
tons and got healthy again. When he was well he was moved	186
back to his new home in the ocean. He was so big he had to be	202
flown in a special plane with a pool that took up the entire inside	216
of the plane.	219
Keiko's new home is in a pen in the ocean, not a tank.	232
Trainers are helping him learn to catch his own fish. Someday	243
they hope he will be released into the wild again. Maybe he will	256
find his original family of Orcas. *94% accuracy*	262

Retell: _____ ORF Total: __58__

Retell Total: __39__

3. Which phonics and word recognition skills should be emphasized in instruction?

Once it seems likely that a student needs to work on phonics and decoding, *a diagnostic decoding survey*, or *diagnostic phonics survey*, will give specific information about the sound-symbol associations the student has learned and those that need to be taught or practiced. A phonics survey samples the reading of words with the most common spelling patterns presented in a logical sequence. That sequence is broadly outlined in Carol Tolman's hourglass figure (*Figure 3.2*), which was introduced in Chapter 2 of this module.

Figure 3.2 The Hourglass Concept of Language Skill Progression
(Contributed by Carol Tolman, used with permission.)

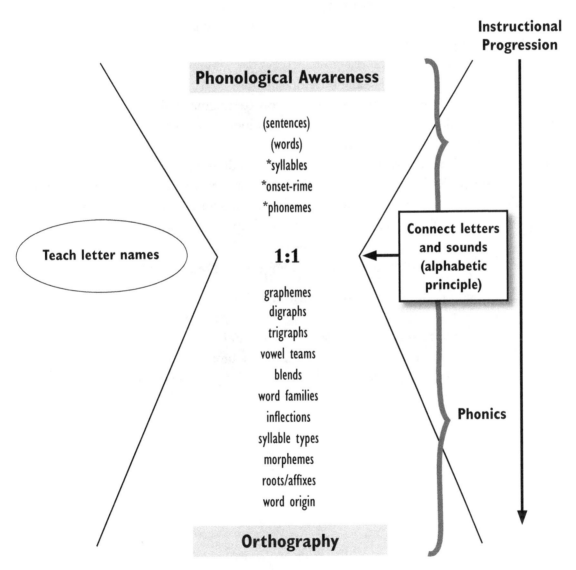

★ Phonology steps most supported by research to improve reading and spelling skills

Several well-constructed, published surveys of decoding skills are readily available for teachers' use. They take little time to administer individually and are necessary to pinpoint where instruction in word-reading *accuracy* should be focused. For your use, we have included an informal survey of decoding and reading skills in *Appendix B* (LETRS Phonics and Word-Reading Survey). Other recommended diagnostic surveys of decoding skills are:

- *Beginning Decoding Survey and Advanced Decoding Survey*, by Really Great Reading Company
  Web site: http://www.rgrco.com/resources/tools/diagnostic-decoding-surveys
- *Phonics Screener for Intervention*™, by 95 Percent Group Inc., 2006
  Web site: http://www.95percentgroup.com
- *Quick Phonics Screener*, by Jan Hasbrouck, distributed by Read Naturally
  Web site: http://www.readnaturally.com
- *CORE Phonics Survey*, by the Consortium on Reading Excellence
  Web site: http://www.corelearn.com

More in–depth (and expensive) diagnostic tests of decoding include:

- *Gallistel-Ellis Test of Coding Skills* by Montage Press
  Web site: http://www.montagepressatibi.com/testingmaterials.htm
- Decoding Skills Test (DST) by Western Psychological Services
  Web site: http://wpspublish.com

A brief, economical, and useful set of diagnostic decoding surveys has been developed by Farrell and Hunter (2007) for Really Great Reading Company. Seven alternate forms (A–G) are contained in the set. Form A is reproduced on the following pages and is distributed free on request by the Really Great Reading Company (http://www.rgrco.com).

Case Study: Interpreting a Diagnostic Decoding Survey

In the diagnostic decoding survey shown in *Figure 3.3* (in *Exercise 3.2*, following), administered to the same third-grader who read the passage in *Figure 3.1*, the error types are tabulated across real word, nonsense word, and sentence reading tasks. *Exercise 3.2* requires you to look closely at the patterns in the protocol (the record form and its notations) in order to make inferences about the student's instructional needs.

Exercise 3.2 | Interpret a Brief Diagnostic Survey of Decoding Skills

- Look carefully at the student's responses, marked on the protocols in *Figure 3.3* on page 81, and the tally of errors. Then answer these questions:

Beginning Decoding Survey (*Figure 3.3*, page 81)

1. Of the first 20 words, is there a difference among sets? Why might the student read the first set of words accurately and make so many errors on words 6–20?

   _____

   _____

2. When the student misreads a word, does he produce a real word or a nonsense word? Does this suggest anything about the student?

   _____

   _____

3. How do you explain this student's "**b**" and "**d**" confusion, and what can be done about it with a third-grader?

   _____

   _____

4. Look at the words where sounds are added. What are those sounds? (What class of phonemes appears to be problematic or elusive?)

   _____

   _____

5. Look at the words where sounds are omitted. Where are those sounds? What are those sounds? Do these errors indicate a phonological processing problem?

   _____

   _____

   _____

(continued)

Exercise 3.2 (continued)

6. How do you describe the student's substitution of *point* for **pond**? In what way does this suggest a phonological processing problem?

_____

_____

7. How do you describe the student's substitution of *thin* for **thid**? In what way does this suggest a phonological processing problem?

_____

_____

8. Does the student make more errors on initial consonant sounds or final consonant sounds? Why might those errors be more common?

_____

_____

Advanced Decoding Survey (refer to Consonant and Vowel Charts on page 82 and *Figure 3.4* on page 83)

9. What speech sounds are typically added or omitted when errors are made?

_____

_____

10. This student is a third-grader but has not mastered or internalized skills often taught in first grade. Do you think that phonics instruction to address those weak underlying skills should be a priority or that it is too late to do anything about the problem?

_____

_____

_____

_____

Exercise 3.2 (continued)

Figure 3.3 Beginning Decoding Survey Results, Third-Grade Student

Student ~~Adam~~

Grade **3**   Date **1-25**

Examiner **LF**

BEGINNING DECODING SURVEY   RECORDING FORM **A**

Error Grid

Observations
Check the appropriate boxes:
☐ Reads sound by sound, then blends word
☒ Possible b/d or b/p reversal
☐ Quick to guess
☐ Slow

	Real Words	No Try	Sight Word	Sound Added or Omitted	Consonant Initial	Consonant Final	Short Vowel	Digraph/Blend
Sight Words	1 see ✓							
	2 one ✓							
	3 they ✓							
	4 you ✓							
	5 are ✓							
CVC Words	6 rag *range*		NA	X		X	X	
	7 lid *little*		NA	XX		X		Consonant Digraph: ch, sh, ck, wh, th
	8 dot *don't*		NA	X			X	
	9 hum ✓		NA					
	10 bet *but*		NA				X	Letters qu
Digraphs & Short Vowels	11 rich ✓		NA			NA		
	12 shop ✓		NA		NA			
	13 tack ✓		NA			NA		
	14 quit ✓		NA			NA		
	15 moth *month*		NA	X		NA	X	Blend
Blends & Short Vowels	16 dust *bust*		NA		X		NA	
	17 step *ship*		NA	X	X		X	NA / X
	18 trip ✓		NA				NA	
	19 pond *point*		NA			X	X	NA / X
	20 brag *bags*		NA				NA	X

Sentences (irregularly spelled sight words are in *italics*)

21–26 *The* cat ~~hid~~ (had/se) in ~~a~~ (the) box.   → Sight Word X | Short Vowel X | NA | NA

27–35 *The* fresh fish *is* still on *the* wet ~~grass~~ (glass).   → No Try X | Sight Word X | Blend X

36–42 Six ~~flat~~ (flags) shells *were* in *my* bath. (flags/shell)   → Sound Added or Omitted XX | Consonant XX

	Nonsense Words	No Try	Sight Word	Sound Added or Omitted	Initial Cons.	Final Cons.	Short Vowel	Digraph	Blend
CVC	43 vop ✓		NA					NA	NA
	44 yud *yub*		NA			X		NA	NA
	45 zin ✓		NA					NA	NA
	46 keb *kib*		NA				X	NA	NA
Digraphs	47 shap *sharp*		NA		NA		X		NA
	48 thid *thin*		NA		NA	X			NA
	49 chut ✓		NA		NA				NA
	50 weck *wech*		NA					X	NA

30	Words Read Correctly (out of 50 total)	Error Column Totals	1	2	8	2	7	9	1	4
			No Try	Sight Word	Sound Added or Omitted	Initial Consonant	Final	Short Vowel	Digraph & Letters qu	Blend

(continued)

Exercise 3.2 (continued)

Consonant and Vowel Sounds Charts

	Lips Together	Teeth on Lip	Tongue Between Teeth	Tongue on Ridge Behind Teeth	Tongue Pulled Back on Roof of Mouth	Back of Throat	Glottis
Stops							
Unvoiced	/p/			/t/		/k/	
Voiced	/b/			/d/		/g/	
Nasals	/m/			/n/		/ng/	
Fricatives							
Unvoiced		/f/	/th/	/s/	/sh/		
Voiced		/v/	/th/	/z/	/zh/		
Affricates							
Unvoiced					/ch/		
Voiced					/j/		
Glides							
Unvoiced						/wh/	/h/
Voiced					/y/	/w/	
Liquids				/l/	/r/		

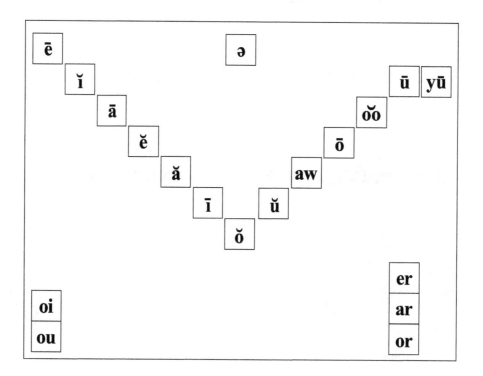

Exercise 3.2 (continued)

Figure 3.4 Advanced Decoding Survey Results, Third-Grade Student

Student _~~Anna~~_

Date _1 - 25_

ADVANCED DECODING SURVEY

RECORDING FORM **A**

Observations
Check the appropriate boxes:
- ☐ Reads sound by sound, then blends word
- ☒ Possible b/d or b/p reversal
- ☐ Quick to guess
- ☐ Slow

Nonsense Words		No Try	Sound Added or Omitted	Consonant Initial	Consonant Final	Short Vowel	Consonant Digraph: sh, ch, th, ph Trigraph: dge, tch	Blend	Advanced Vowel
1	fut ✓								
2	shab *shup*			NA	X	X			
3	thox ✓			NA					
4	lutch *lunch*			X	NA				
5	phim ✓			NA					
6	gred ✓						NA		
7	strob *stob*			X			NA	X	Advanced Vowel
8	misp ✓						NA		
9	yume *yummy*		X		NA	NA	NA	NA	X
10	weag *weg*				NA	NA	NA	NA	X
11	jaib *jib*				NA	NA	NA	NA	X
12	soam *sloam*		X		NA	NA	NA	NA	
13	foom ✓				NA	NA	NA	NA	
14	vawk ✓				NA	NA	NA	NA	
15	soid ✓				NA	NA	NA	NA	
16	zout ✓				NA	NA	NA	NA	
17	foy ✓				NA	NA	NA	NA	
18	fird ✓				NA	NA	NA		
19	gorf ✓				NA	NA	NA		
20	lerm ✓				NA	NA	NA		
Error Column Totals		0	4	0	1	1	0	1	3
		No Try	Sound Added or Omitted	Initial Consonant	Final Consonant	Short Vowel	Digraph & Trigraph	Blend	Advanced Vowel

Side labels: One Syllable & One Vowel / VCE / Vowel Teams / Vowel + R

Multi-Syllable Words

Nonsense Words		Incorrect or No Try		Real Words		Incorrect or No Try
21	kimplut ✓			26	fantastic ✓	
22	gruckle *druckle*	X		27	several ✓	
23	slafnode *snifate*	X		28	attached ✓	
24	dirper *dripper*	X		29	recognize *receive*	X
25	panventic *panvest*	X		30	lotion *location*	X
Multi-Syllable Nonsense Word Errors		4		**Multi-Syllable Real Word Errors**		2

_17_ **Words Read Correctly** (out of 30 total)

4. Does the student need intervention in spelling and writing?

Students with reading difficulties also will struggle with one or more aspects of writing. Some students are affected by specific writing disabilities (dysgraphia) even though their reading is progressing satisfactorily (Berninger & Wolf, 2009). Spelling can be assessed in several ways:

- A standardized test with normative data, such as the *Test of Written Spelling* (Pro-Ed);
- A comprehensive assessment of writing skills, using a rubric within a standardized test, such as the *Test of Written Language* (Pro-Ed);
- Error analysis in writing samples; and/or
- A **diagnostic spelling inventory**.

A diagnostic spelling inventory will show which spelling conventions a student has learned along a progression of orthographic knowledge. Two levels of a qualitative spelling inventory are offered for your use in *Appendix C,* along with case studies to practice scoring the inventories.

Case Study: Spelling Inventory Results

Our third-grade student's spelling samples on the next page and Primary Spelling Inventory results (*Figure 3.5,* on page 86) follow. If you are unfamiliar with the inventory and how it is scored, take a few minutes to go to *Appendix C* and practice scoring the spelling inventories of the second-grade students whose results are given. Then, look closely at this student's results. After tallying up the feature totals, you can easily see the phoneme-grapheme correspondences that the student knows, those that need some review, and those that need to be taught as new concepts.

(Please note that this examiner forgot to add an extra point to the feature totals when the word was correct. This scoring difference, however, will not affect the observations you can make while you answer the questions in *Exercise 3.3.*)

Spelling Samples

1	fan	
2	pet	
3	dig	
4	mob	
5	rope	
6	wafe	wait
7	chunk	
8	<u>sed</u>	sled
9	stik	stick
10	sin	shine
11	drem	dream
12	blad	blade
13	cowch	coach
14	frit	fright
15	shaeng	
16	tokt	talked
17	camping	
18	thorn	
19	shawtod	shouted
20	spowed	spoil
21	growl	
22	cerp	chirp
23	clapped	
24	trip	tries
25	hiking	

Figure 3.5   Primary Spelling Inventory and Inventory Results, Third-Grade Student

	Initial consonant	Final consonant	Digraph	Blend	Short vowel	Long vowel (VCe)	Vowel Team/ Diphthong	r-controlled vowel	Inflections	Whole word correct?	Word totals
1. fan	f	n			a					–	4
2. pet	p	t			e					–	4
3. dig	d	g			i					–	4
4. mob	m	b			o					–	4
5. rope	r	p				o_e				–	4
6. wait	w	t					ai				2
7. chunk			ch	nk	u					–	4
8. sled				sl	e						1
9. stick		-ck		st	i						2
10. shine			sh			i_e					0
11. dream				dr			ea				1
12. blade				bl		a_e					1
13. coach			-ch				oa				1
14. fright				fr			igh				1
15. snowing				sn			ow		-ing	–	4
16. talked							-al		-ed		0
17. camping				-mp					-ing	–	3
18. thorn			th					or		–	3
19. shouted			sh				ou				1
20. spoil				sp			oi				1
21. growl				gr			ow			–	3
22. chirp			ch					ir			0
23. clapped				cl					-pped	–	3
24. tries				tr					-es	–	1
25. hiking									-king	–	2
FEATURE TOTALS	6/6	6/7	4/6	11/12	7/7	1/3	2/9	1/2	4/6	12/25	54/81

Exercise 3.3 | Spelling Inventory Analysis and Comparison With Decoding Survey

- Looking at the Primary Spelling Inventory score sheet in *Figure 3.5*, note answers to these questions:

  1. What elements does the student spell accurately?

  _____

  2. What features or correspondences require some review?

  _____

  3. What correspondence patterns must be taught as new or unknown concepts?

  _____

- Looking back at the beginning decoding survey results (*Figure 3.3*, page 81), formulate answers to these questions:

  1. Is there a difference between the student's ability to read versus spell words with short vowels?

  _____

  2. Is there a difference between the student's ability to read versus spell words with consonant blends?

  _____

  3. At what point in the scope and sequence of code instruction do the skills of word-reading and spelling seem to converge for this student?

  _____

  4. What could account for the differences between encoding (spelling) and decoding accuracy?

  _____

  _____

  5. If your hypothesis is correct, how would that information influence your approach to instruction?

  _____

  _____

  _____

  _____

Qualitative Analysis of Spelling Errors

Spelling errors also reveal something about the underlying language processes that are affecting student performance. Typical errors are explained in Modules 2 and 3 of LETRS and are also discussed in depth in Moats (2010) and Moats and Rosow (2010). Broadly speaking, four levels of language organization are processed during spelling. Errors can be analyzed in terms of their:

- phonological (or phonetic) accuracy;
- orthographic accuracy;
- morphological accuracy; and
- syntactic accuracy.

Table 3.1 (next page) contains examples of each kind of structural linguistic error, drawn from many student writing samples.

Table 3.1　Spelling Errors at Four Levels of Language Structure

Level of Language Structure	Definition	Examples
Phonetics (Phonology)	Speech sounds are omitted or added; substitutions show misperception of the features of phonemes or phoneme sequences.	• Confusion of sounds that share articulatory features: BAF/**bath**; FLASE/**flesh**; INEMS/**items** • Voicing substitutions: JILLE/**chili**; DISCOFR/**discover** • Misplacement, omission of liquids /l/ and /r/: TEER/**tree**; COROL/**color**; THOWING/**throwing**; STAT/**start** • Omission of nasals after vowels and before consonants: WET/**went**; GRAP/**gramp** • Omission or substitution of schwa (unaccented syllable): FRIGHTING/**frightening** • Omission of consonants, especially in blends: PAT/**plant**; FIGHT/**fright**; MOT/**most**; FRAS/**friends** • Inaccurate vowel: FASH/**fresh**; SPART/**sport**; TAC/**took**; FRAS/**friends**
Orthography	Speech sounds are represented—especially the correct number and sequence—but graphemes are incorrect. Sometimes letter names are used for sounds.	• Using acceptable but wrong grapheme: LIMOW/**limo**; UV/**of**; WHIE/**why**; HER/**here**; PICH/**pitch** • Misspelling schwa vowels: MAMITH/**mammoth** • Homophone substitutions: ARE/**our**; NO/**know**; RIGHT/**rite/write**; BRIDLE/**bridal**
Morphology	Compound parts misspelled. Inflections omitted or spelled phonetically. Prefixes, roots, and suffixes misspelled.	SUMTHING/**something**; DRAGD/**dragged**; ECKSPERIENS/**experience**; PROGECT/**project**; FINELY/**finally**; UNEKORN/**unicorn**
Grammatical/ Syntactic	Spelling does not match the part of speech (syntactic role) of the word.	PAST/**passed** YOUR/**you're** THERE/**they're** ITS/**it's**

Exercise 3.4 | Explain Spelling Errors

- Look closely at the spelling errors (all capital letters) in the "Examples" column of *Table 3.1* (previous page). Within the list of spelling errors, identify exactly what the student is confusing about phonemes, graphemes, syllables, morphemes, or grammatical role of a word.

- You may need to review the speech sound charts (LETRS Module 2, 2nd Edition, pp. 34 and 39) and the information in LETRS Module 3 to find which spelling errors listed in *Table 3.1* are examples of the following confusions:

1. Spelling a compound word phonetically without regard to the free morphemes that compose it:

   _____

2. Showing the "slide" in the long vowel /ī/:

   _____

3. Omitting a liquid consonant in a beginning blend:

   _____

4. Misspelling a common Latin root:

   _____

5. Substituting one fricative consonant phoneme for another:

   _____

6. Not knowing the position-based spelling pattern for an affricate after a short vowel:

   _____

7. Substituting a front short vowel for another that is adjacent on the vowel articulation chart:

   _____

8. Misspelling a common Latin prefix:

   _____

9. Confusing a possessive and a contraction:

   _____

10. A homophone error that could be corrected if the base word's adjective suffix and meaning were recognized in the word's structure:

    _____

Linguistic processing errors such as the ones in *Exercise 3.4* are important to notice because they point to specific targets for instruction. A student who cannot track the sounds in words needs to get help with phoneme awareness. The student who reliably tracks the sounds in words, but who can't remember basic graphemes and grapheme sequences, needs foundational instruction in the orthographic code. The student who is good at basic phonics but oblivious to the meaningful parts in words and the grammatical role of a word in a sentence is ready to benefit from a strong emphasis on morphology and word origin. This general progression—a "nutshell" version of *Table 3.3* (following)—is represented in *Table 3.2*.

Table 3.2 Progression of Word Study Through the Elementary Grades

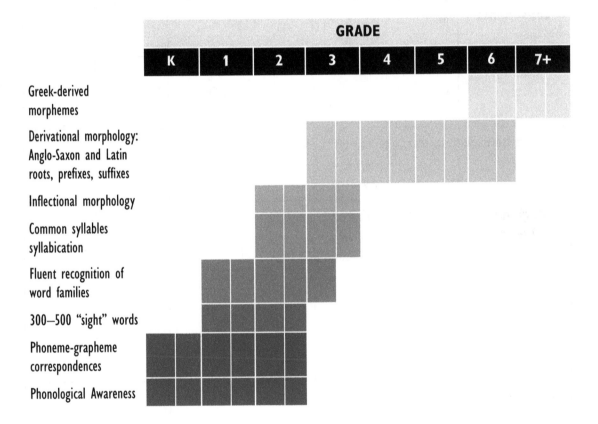

Classroom spelling programs with a strong emphasis on understanding language structure rather than memorization (Joshi, Treiman, Carreker, & Moats, 2008-9) are *Primary Spelling by Pattern, Level 1* (Javernick & Moats, 2006) and *Level 2* (Hooper & Moats, 2011). See *Table 3.3* (next two pages) for a scope and sequence of spelling instruction by grade level.

Table 3.3 Scope and Sequence for Spelling Instruction

INSTRUCTION	GRADE LEVEL					
	1	**2**	**3**	**4**	**5**	**6**
Beginning consonants	b c d f g h j k l m n p qu r s t v w y z	qu-, ce-, ci-, cy-, ge-, gi-, gy-				
Ending consonants	b d g m n p t x	-ff, -ll, -ss, -zz, -x, -ve, -ck, -ng	-ge, -dge			
Digraphs	ch, sh, th, wh	-ch, -tch ph, ch, gh		ph, gh in Greek words		
Ending blends	-st, -ft	-mp, -nd, -nt, -lf, -lt, -nk				
Beginning blends	bl-, cl- fl-, gl-, pl-, sl-, br-, cr-, dr-, fr-, gr-, pr-, tr-, sc-, sk-, sl-, sm-, sn-, sp-, st-, sw-	scr-, spr-, squ-, spl-, str-, tw-	shr-, thr-	sch-		
Silent-letter spellings		kn, -lk	wr, gn	ps, rh		
Vowels	a, e, i, o, u (short); a_e, o_e, u_e, i_e	**y** as long **i** **y** as long **e**	Schwa in two-syllable words; eigh, ough	**y** as short **i**		
Vowel teams	ee, ai, ay, oa, ea	ou, ow, oi, oy, au, aw, oo, eu, ew, igh	oo (**foot**) ui, ei, ie			

INSTRUCTION	GRADE LEVEL					
	1	**2**	**3**	**4**	**5**	**6**
Vowel-r	or, ar, er	er, ir, ur; war, wor	err, ear, air, oar			
Inflectional suffixes	-s, -ed, -ing (no change in base word)	-s, -ed, -ing (doubling and drop-**e** rules)	-er, -est (comparative); Change **y** to **i** rule	When rules do and do not apply	Advanced doubling rule	
Prefixes			un-, re-	pre-, en-, dis-, mis-, ex-, in-	con-, per-, com-, ad-, a- (chameleon prefixes)	bi-, mal-, circum-, inter-, intra-, super-, trans-
Derivational suffixes		-en, -hood, -ly	-ment, -less, -ful, -ness	-tion, -sion, -ture, -able, -ous, -ic, -al	-age, -ace, -ary, -ence, -ity, -ation	-ology, -osity, -itis, -scope, -plasm
Contractions	I'm, it's, don't	he'll, they've, you're, we'd				
Syllable/ Morpheme patterns	Concept of a syllable	Compounds; words with closed, open, and CV**e** syllables	Compounds; the two syllable types	Morphemes override syllables	Latin morphemes (roots)	Greek combining forms

Writing Sample Analysis

A writing sample will also indicate how well a student can compose a narrative or expository text and how well the basic skills of transcription—handwriting, spelling, punctuation, organization of the work on the page—are developing. Although objective measurement of writing is difficult and rubrics that require rater judgment can be unreliable, writing samples always provide some valuable information about a student's developing skills with language. We will tackle issues of writing assessment and instruction in Module 9 but, at this point, we encourage teachers to keep samples of students' writing and make informal observations about them.

Case Study: Analysis of Written Composition

The following is our third-grader's written composition about his "dream house." Read his story, check the translation and, after making your own observations, tackle the questions in *Exercise 3.5*.

Writing Sample

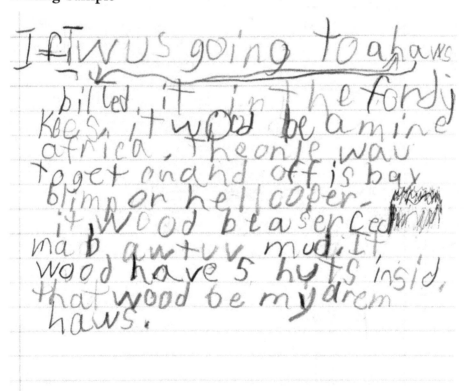

Translation: If I was going to build a house it [would be] in the Florida Keys. It would be a mini-Africa. The only way to get on and off is by blimp or helicopter. It would be a circle made out of mud. It would have five huts inside. That would be my dream house.

Exercise 3.5 Reconcile Reading, Spelling, and Writing Results

- After reviewing this student's ORF passage score (*Figure 3.1* on page 76), beginning and advanced decoding survey results (*Figures 3.3* and *3.4* on pages 81 and 83), spelling inventory results (*Figure 3.5* on page 86), and writing sample (previous page), answer these questions as well as you can:

1. Are there high-frequency words misspelled in the writing sample that the student could read accurately in the passage? What might account for this discrepancy?

   _____

   _____

   _____

   _____

2. In spite of this student's ability to invent phonetic spellings for words, there is evidence in the diagnostic tasks of a lingering weakness in phonological processing. What can you point to that indicates a weakness in phonological processing?

   _____

   _____

3. Using the diagnostic evidence obtained so far, what skills and concepts would this student's lessons need to address?

   _____

   _____

   _____

   _____

Standardized and Computer-Based Assessments of Spelling

Standardized tests of spelling ability show where a student stands in relation to other students of his age or grade level. These assessments may be used to verify whether a student's problems merit special instruction or not. Commonly used and well standardized tests include:

- Test of Written Spelling, 4th Edition (TWS-4) (Pro-Ed)
  Web site: http://www.proedinc.com
- Wide Range Achievement Test, 4th Edition (WRAT-4) (Pro-Ed)
  Web site: http://www.proedinc.com
- Wechsler Individual Achievement Test®, 3rd Edition (WIAT®-III) (Psychological Corporation)
  Web site: http://www.pearsonassessments.com
- Test of Written Language, 4th Edition (TOWL-4) (Pro-Ed)
  Web site: http://www.proedinc.com

Technology-based assessments include:

- SpellDoctor™
  Web site: http://www.spelldoctor.com
- Spelling Performance Evaluation for Language & Literacy (SPELL-2)
  Web site: http://www.learningbydesign.com
- Super Spell Assessment Disk
  Web site: http://www.4mation.co.uk/cat/spelling.html

5. Do I need to assess phonological skills directly, and does the instructional program or lesson framework need to focus on phoneme awareness (i.e., phoneme identity, blending, and segmentation)?

Whether to spend time and resources giving students additional tests for phonological processing and/or phoneme awareness is a judgment call on the part of the teacher/specialist team. Tests of phonological processing do not always have the straightforward relationship with reading that we would like (Hogan, Catts, & Little, 2005). Additional direct assessment is indicated when a student's reading, spelling, writing, and language problems are relatively pronounced and there are good reasons to document an underlying phonological processing weakness. Those reasons include:

- a low score on a brief screening test (e.g., PSF) that should be corroborated;
- documentation that the student's program should include explicit teaching of phonological skills; and
- evaluation of language functions for the purpose of classification of a learning disorder.

Direct assessment of phonological processing is accomplished with auditory-verbal tasks. If the assessment requires the manipulation of print, it is a test of phonics or spelling—not a direct measure of phonology.

Measures of phonological processing often have a rapidly changing predictive relationship with reading. At different points in reading development, they have different statistical relationships with overall reading skill. Phonological awareness assessments can be weak-to-strong predictors of reading and spelling, depending on when they are given and what they measure. Phoneme segmentation, for example, predicts reading most reliably at the mid-kindergarten to mid-first grade level. Rhyming is not a great predictor of reading or spelling at any age. Phoneme deletion is too hard for young students to be meaningful, but deletion tasks can elicit any remaining or subtle weaknesses affecting a second- or third-grader. If direct diagnostic assessment of phonological skill is undertaken, test(s) should be used with an understanding of their reliability and predictive validity for a specific population at a specific point in reading development.

Commercially published measures of phonological awareness that are often used in research and clinical work include:

- Lindamood Auditory Conceptualization Test, 3rd Edition (LAC-3)
  Web site: http://www.pearsonassessments.com
- Comprehensive Test of Phonological Processing (CTOPP)
  Web site: http://www.proedinc.com
- Test of Phonological Awareness, 2nd Edition: PLUS (TOPA-2+)
  Web site: http://www.linguisystems.com
- Phonological Awareness Literacy Screening (PALS™)
  Web site: http://pals.virginia.edu
- Woodcock Johnson® III Normative Update (NU) Tests of Cognitive Abilities
  Web site: http://www.riverpub.com
- The Phonological Awareness Test 2 (PAT-2)
  Web site: http://www.linguisystems.com
- Test of Auditory Analysis Skills (TAAS)
  Web site: http://www.academictherapy.com

Exercise 3.6 | Role-Play a Phonological Awareness Screener

- With a partner, role-play administration of these 15 pretend items that are modeled after the Test of Auditory Analysis Skills, published first in 1975 by the Walker Educational Book Corporation in Jerome Rosner's (1975) *Helping Children Overcome Learning Difficulties.* (The actual 40-item test is currently available from Academic Therapy Publications.)

1.	"Say **batboy**."	"Now say it again, but don't say **boy**."	**bat**
2.	"Say **houseboat**."	"Now say it again, but don't say **house**."	**boat**
3.	"Say **sunroof**."	"Now say it again, but don't say **roof**."	**sun**
4.	"Say **napkin**."	"Now say it again, but don't say **nap**."	**kin**
5.	"Say **banana**."	"Now say it again, but don't say **ba**."	**nana**
6.	"Say **goat**."	"Now say it again, but don't say /g/."	**oat**
7.	"Say **seat**."	"Now say it again, but don't say /s/."	**eat**
8.	"Say **make**."	"Now say it again, but don't say /m/."	**ache**
9.	"Say **dame**."	"Now say it again, but don't say /m/."	**day**
10.	"Say **rode**."	"Now say it again, but don't say /d/."	**row**
11.	"Say **choose**."	"Now say it again, but don't say /z/."	**chew**
12.	"Say **slap**."	"Now say it again, but don't say /s/."	**lap**
13.	"Say **pray**."	"Now say it again, but don't say /p/."	**ray**
14.	"Say **stake**."	"Now say it again, but don't say /t/."	**sake**
15.	"Say **smell**."	"Now say it again, but don't say /m/."	**sell**

Exercise 3.7
(optional)

Identify and Compare the Content of Phonological Assessments

- Measures of phonological processing and phonological awareness differ a great deal in the range of tasks, complexity of tasks, and predictive validity of tasks. If you have access to several PA screening assessments and diagnostic assessments, check what each of them measures in the table below. To do this, you will need to be very familiar with the aspects of phonological processing that are presented in Module 2 of LETRS.

- Consider these questions as you compare the assessments:
  1. Which assessment(s) are designed for quick screening? For in-depth evaluation?
  2. Which assessment(s) are wide-ranging? Which are focused on one specific skill?
  3. Which assessment(s) are accompanied by research data or references regarding validity and reliability?

Phonological Task	Assessment #1	Assessment #2	Assessment #3
Segmenting sentences into words or counting words in sentences			
Rhyme recognition			
Rhyme production			
Syllable segmentation and/or blending			
Onset-rime segmentation and/or blending			
Odd word out (Which word does not begin/end with the same sound?)			
Word discrimination (Are these the same or different?)			
Phoneme isolation (Say the first sound of this word.)			
Phoneme blending			
Phoneme segmentation			
Phoneme substitution			
Phoneme deletion			
Word repetition			
List memory (digits, words)			
Sentence memory			
Rapid automatic naming (RAN) or rapid serial naming			

The point of *Exercise 3.7* is that many measures exist for the purpose of assessing "phonological awareness," but when you really look at what is in them, they differ considerably. While we advise that you use these measures selectively, and with an understanding of what they measure, we also assume that most students benefit from systematic and informed instruction about speech sounds in the context of reading, spelling, and vocabulary lessons. Good instruction is going to draw students' attention to spoken and written language structure and meaning.

6. Do my data make sense so far?

After you have gathered diagnostic information on a student's screening results and word recognition, phonics, spelling, and phonological skills, it's time to sit back and take stock. Do the results present a consistent picture of strengths and weaknesses? All educational and psychological measurements contain some degree of error; no one measure is a perfect indicator of a student's "true" abilities. However, information obtained from assessments, work samples, and observations should converge into a pattern. If there is no pattern, then the student's needs have probably not been reliably assessed. Options in this phase of assessment include:

- Retesting to corroborate earlier results.
- Cross-referencing assessments; giving another measure of the same skill area.
- Referring the student to other professional(s) from related disciplines, such as speech and language or psychology.

Case Study: Composite Diagnostic Test Results

The student in our case study earned the following pretest and posttest scores after 10 weeks of intensive (4 hours a day) instruction at a reading clinic. Instruction focused on decoding, spelling, and comprehension.

Skill Assessed	Assessment Tool	Scores (percentile)	
		Pre-Intervention December	Post-Intervention April
Vocabulary	Peabody Picture Vocabulary Test–Third Edition (PPVT-III)	98th	98th
Phonological Awareness	Lindamood Auditory Conceptualization Test (LAC-3)	25th	32nd
Oral Reading	Gray Oral Reading Test—Fourth Edition (GORT-4)		
	Rate	2nd	5th
	Accuracy	1st	16th
	Fluency	1st	5th
	Comprehension	9th	16th
	Slosson Oral Reading Test-Revised (SORT-R3)	3rd	9th
Written Language	Test of Written Language-3 (TOWL-3)		
	Contextual Conventions	9th	16th
	Contextual Language	9th	37th
	Story Construction	37th	37th
	Spontaneous Writing	10th	23rd

Overall, the student made some progress in this remedial program, but the reading, spelling, and writing scores show that he was consistently in the lower quartile (the bottom 25%) in reading fluency and accuracy, well below his strong oral language and verbal comprehension abilities. His reading comprehension is limited by severe problems with basic reading skill, not by his oral language comprehension, which is a clear strength. His weaknesses in phoneme sequencing were pronounced in relation to his superior vocabulary. These results are very consistent with the diagnostic survey results, showing that in spite of intensive remediation, the student still struggles with decoding accuracy and fluency. His spelling reflects both phonological processing and orthographic memory problems that need to be addressed with ongoing, intensive instruction.

Diagnostic Assessment of Vocabulary and Oral/Written Language Comprehension

> ### Recommendation
>
> *Routinely check comprehension of any student who is below benchmark or who demonstrates comprehension problems in the classroom using formal and informal observation, interview, work products, and tests.*

Diagnostic assessment of vocabulary, oral language production, verbal comprehension, and reading comprehension is much more problematic than the measurement of decoding, reading fluency, or spelling. This is true for several reasons:

- The domain of vocabulary and language comprehension is very broad and can be difficult to define for the purposes of measurement. Comprehension is not a single skill, and the comprehension demands of reading change from grade to grade.
- The subskills or components of comprehension are not easily identified, separated from one another, and measured reliably; thus, tests seldom agree about the "breakdown" of component comprehension skills, and it is difficult to know the implications of single test results for instruction.
- Language comprehension and vocabulary tests tend to be time-consuming, and the payoff for administering them may be relatively low in terms of instructional guidance.
- Language comprehension and vocabulary tests often require special training to administer and score.
- Language comprehension and vocabulary tests may be labeled similarly but may measure different aspects of comprehension and have low correlations with one another (Cutting & Scarborough, 2006; Keenan, Betjemann, & Olson, 2008).

Research Summary

Keenan, J., Betjemann, R. S., & Olson, R. K. (2008) Reading comprehension tests vary in the skills they assess: Differential dependence on decoding and oral comprehension. *Scientific Studies of Reading, 12*(3), 281–300.

Comprehension tests are often used interchangeably, suggesting an implicit assumption that they are measuring the same thing. We ... compar[e] some of the most popular reading comprehension measures. The Gray Oral Reading Test (GORT), the two assessments (retellings and comprehension questions) from the Qualitative Reading Inventory (QRI), the Woodcock-Johnson Passage Comprehension subtest (WJPC), and the Reading Comprehension test from the Peabody Individual Achievement Test (PIAT). Modest intercorrelations among the tests suggested that they were measuring different skills. ... We discuss the serious implications for research and clinical practice of having different comprehension tests measure different skills and of having the same test assess different skills depending on developmental level.

What then is the best way to check and observe comprehension? First, remember that ORF, maze passages, and standardized tests in which students read passages and answer questions can be very good indicators of overall reading proficiency. Reading comprehension and vocabulary are assessed indirectly by those screening and outcome tests, though they do not tell you how to approach instruction. You may still need to figure out more specifically what kind of help the student needs.

Before undertaking a time-consuming set of diagnostic tests, a teacher or team should try the RIOT approach (Howell, Hosp, & Hosp, in press):

R*eview* – school records, work samples, health history.

I*nterview* – the student, the parents, other teachers.

O*bserve* – whether comprehension problems occur in all school subjects and in all topic areas.

T*est* – using curriculum-based tests of skills, concepts, and strategies taught.

Relying on Informal Observation

When students have problems with comprehension, in addition to knowing whether the student can read the words with sufficient speed and accuracy, we generally want to find answers to the following questions:

Q: Does the student have trouble with comprehension of both spoken and written language?

   Strategy for assessment: Try reading passages aloud to the student and see if he/she can answer the questions orally. Determine if problems occur across most subject areas.

Q: Does the student lack exposure to background knowledge and literate language?

   Strategy for assessment: Look for understanding that varies greatly depending on the subject matter. Check comprehension under conditions in which background knowledge is provided rather than assumed.

Q: Are ELL students unfamiliar with English vocabulary and syntax?

Strategy for assessment: Assess the student in his/her first language to see if a discrepancy exists. Look at results of English language mastery assessments.

Q: Can the student monitor his/her own comprehension?

Strategy for assessment: Observe whether the student "reads over" errors or stops to correct them. Check comprehension when the student reads aloud with feedback vs. reading silently.

Q: Can the student interpret complex syntax?

Strategy for assessment: Check to see if shortening sentences or rephrasing complex language helps the student to understand the meanings.

Q: Is the student attentive to details in the text?

Strategy for assessment: Query the student frequently during shared oral reading. Can the student recognize implied (under the surface) meanings in the text base? Does the student notice detail and make "gap-filling" inferences?

Q: Has the student constructed an accurate mental model of the text's meanings after reading carefully?

Strategy for assessment: Ask the student to retell, paraphrase, or summarize what he/she has read.

Q: Can the student remember information read previously?

Strategy for assessment: Ask the student to keep notes, journals, diagrams, and/or illustrations of key information and to revisit those prompts periodically. Do those aids help with recall?

In-Depth, Multidisciplinary Diagnostic Evaluation

This module is not a complete course for learning specialists or clinicians, but we have included in *Table 3.5* an outline of the domains that should be included in a comprehensive diagnostic assessment. This list can serve as an overview for student study teams embarking on a comprehensive evaluation. Current references on the science of in-depth diagnostic assessment include Berninger & Wolf (2009), Fletcher et al. (2007), and Pennington (2009).

Table 3.5   Domains Addressed in a Diagnostic Assessment of Reading Disability or Difficulty

Area of Inquiry	Observation, Interview, or Measurement
Family and Individual History	• Family history of reading, writing, or language learning problems • Health or medical impairments? • Developmental delays? • Parents' concerns about speech, language, motor skills, attention span, mood, behavior, or academic progress
Cognitive Ability or Intellectual Functioning (optional for an assessment of learning disabilities)	• WISC-IV (Wechsler Intelligence Scale for Children) or Woodcock Johnson Tests of Cognitive Abilities • Measurement of functioning in processing speed, memory, verbal reasoning, non-verbal reasoning, sustained attention
Specific Language Abilities	• Speech-sound and syllable awareness • Speech-sound and word pronunciation • Word retrieval and naming • Rapid sequential naming of letters, numbers, objects, colors • Knowledge of word meanings (expressive and receptive) • Comprehension and production of syntax • Discourse comprehension (listening) • Organization and production of expressive language
Single-Word Decoding, speech and accuracy	• Real words out of context (timed and untimed) • Nonsense words
Oral Reading Fluency	• Graded oral reading passages, WCPM
Vocabulary	• Recognition of word meanings, multiple-choice response • Production of definitions • Use of words in context
Reading Comprehension	• Summarizing, retelling, answering questions, completing cloze (Maze) passages
Written Composition	• Composition of story or essay • Rubric analysis (ideas, grammar, organization, sentence length and complexity, word choice, voice and style) • Component skills analysis (sentence-writing fluency, sentence combining, paragraph organization, outline of main and supporting ideas)
Spelling	• Developmental spelling inventory • Norm-referenced spelling test (dictated) • Error analysis
Handwriting	• Copying • Alphabet production • Legibility • Handedness, grip, and posture

Summary

Let's take stock at this point. Discuss with colleagues where you and/or your district or school currently stand with regard to the use of outcome, screening, and diagnostic assessments. Give yourself or your school a letter grade (A–F) on assessment practices. If the grade is less than A, explain how you think the practices might be improved.

1. Use of universal screening that is brief, reliable, and valid. **A   B   C   D   F**

   _____

   _____

2. Appropriate use of screening—as a formative assessment, not an outcome or evaluation measure. **A   B   C   D   F**

   _____

   _____

3. Attention to rate and accuracy in oral reading fluency results. **A   B   C   D   F**

   _____

   _____

4. Use of a phonics screener or diagnostic decoding survey to identify gaps in skills.
   A   B   C   D   F

   _____

   _____

5. Use of a diagnostic decoding survey to group students for instruction.
   A   B   C   D   F

   _____

   _____

6. Use of a spelling inventory that corresponds to an instructional sequence.
   A   B   C   D   F

   _____

   _____

7. Application of spelling inventory results to decisions about spelling instruction.
   A   B   C   D   F

   _____

   _____

8. Use of writing samples as formative assessments to help guide instruction.
   A   B   C   D   F

   _____

   _____

9. Selective use of diagnostic phonological awareness assessment. **A   B   C   D   F**

   _____

   _____

10. Use of the RIOT approach to comprehension assessment. **A   B   C   D   F**

    _____

    _____

Chapter 4

Is the Help Helping?

Learner Objectives for Chapter 4

- Tailor intervention plans to student characteristics.
- Understand the purpose of progress-monitoring.
- Know the special features of progress-monitoring assessments.
- Chart ORF data.
- Practice using progress-monitoring results to shape ongoing instructional decisions.

Warm-Up: Where Are You With Progress-Monitoring?

1. How often do you conduct progress-monitoring assessments?

   _____

2. Do you routinely assess the same skills, or do you use different measures for different types of students? **Same   Different**

3. Do your measures have alternate forms? **Yes   No**

4. Are they administered under standardized conditions? **Yes   No**

5. Do you chart the results and share the results with students? **Yes   No**
   With colleagues? **Yes   No**

6. Do you use the results to influence instructional decisions? **Yes   No**

7. What challenges, if any, are you facing in using progress-monitoring?

   _____

   _____

Matching Programs and Approaches With Student Characteristics

As we emphasized in the previous chapter, not all students' instructional needs are alike (e.g., Aaron et al., 2008; Tunmer, 2008). After you have conducted screening and diagnostic assessments and sorted your data, you should be able to identify students whose instructional needs fall into these four broad categories:

1. Weaknesses in word recognition, fluency, and comprehension.
2. Weak phonology and word recognition with good/better language comprehension.
3. Dysfluent reading with accurate word recognition and adequate phonological processing.
4. Poor comprehension with adequate word recognition and phonology.

Weaknesses in word recognition, fluency, and comprehension

As emphasized in previous modules and chapters, the majority of poor readers will need a comprehensive approach to instruction that addresses all strands of the "reading rope." A complete approach includes: (a) practice attending to phonological aspects of words; (b) systematic, direct, cumulative, and explicit teaching of the orthographic code; (c) vocabulary; (d) fluency; and (e) both listening and reading comprehension at the sentence and discourse levels. Spelling and writing are woven into the lessons.

There are many comprehensive programs available from which to choose. Be sure that the program is appropriate for the age, grade, and skill level of the students. Generally speaking, the lower the overall language proficiency of students, the more important it is to teach all aspects of literacy directly, explicitly, and systematically. Examples of comprehensive programs designed for instruction of groups of students at some risk include:

- *Reading Mastery* (SRA/McGraw-Hill)
- *ReadWell* (Cambium/Sopris)
- *Success for All* (Success for All Foundation)
- *Early Reading Intervention* (Pearson Scott Foresman)
- *Preventing Academic Failure*
  Web site: http://www.pafprogram.com

Weak phonology and word recognition with good/better language comprehension

These students, who fit the "classic dyslexic" profile, will respond well to an approach that puts more emphasis on word recognition and phonology—at least until they can read words with sufficient accuracy and fluency to support reading comprehension. Many excellent resources exist for guiding instruction that teaches the structure of spoken and written language at the level of phonemes, graphemes, and morphemes. A complete lesson framework was presented, modeled, and practiced in Module 7 of LETRS. Briefly, the lesson framework included direct teaching of:

- speech sound identity, blending, and segmentation;
- graphemes to represent phonemes, using multisensory techniques;
- decoding and blending of written words from left to right;
- automatic recognition of "outlaw" words;
- understanding of inflectional morphology;
- word and phrase practice for automaticity; and
- application to text-reading.

Among the many excellent programs and resources for teaching phoneme awareness and letter knowledge at grades K and 1 are:

- *Focus on /F/onemes* (K or grade 1)
  Web sites: http://www.focusonfonemes.com or http://thephonicsformula.com
- *Phonemic Awareness in Young Children: A Classroom Curriculum* (Brookes Publishing)
- *Lindamood Phoneme Sequencing® (LiPS®) Program* (Pro-Ed)
- *Road to the Code* (Brookes Publishing)
- *WatchWord* (Cambium/Sopris)
- *Stepping Stones to Literacy* (Cambium/Sopris)

Among the many excellent programs for teaching beginning phonics and decoding in a systematic, explicit, cumulative, multisensory manner, grades 1 and 2, are:

- *Fundations®* (Wilson Language)
- *Phonics and Spelling Through Phoneme-Grapheme Mapping* (Cambium/Sopris)
- *Road to Reading* (Brookes Publishing)
- *Phono-Graphix*
  Web site: http://www.readamerica.net
- *Sound Partners* (Cambium/Sopris)

Those struggling readers who still require intensive instruction in phonics and word recognition at grade 3 are probably candidates for programs such as the following:

- *The Herman Method™* (Revised Edition) (Cambium/Sopris)
- *S.P.I.R.E.®* (Educators Publishing Service)

Dysfluent reading with accurate word recognition and good phonology

A few students stand out because they can segment words orally, spell phonetically, and read words accurately but slowly. Their reading rate, however, is very slow, and they need many exposures to words to develop automatic word recognition. Their lessons are likely to emphasize:

- word structure review, particularly base words with inflectional and derivational morphemes;
- tracing, saying, writing, and remembering high-frequency words;
- 1-minute speed drills on component skills;
- multiple-meaning words and semantic associations;
- preview of vocabulary in a text;
- phrase reading; and
- repeated readings of a text for varied purposes.

Several excellent teaching resources and programs are available to address the needs of this kind of learner; for example:

- *RAVE-O* (for grades 2–5) (Cambium/Sopris)
- *Six-Minute Solution, Primary* (for grades 1–3) (Cambium/Sopris)
- *Great Leaps*
  Web site: http://www.greatleaps.com/
- *Read Naturally*
  Web site: http://www.readnaturally.com/

Poor comprehension with adequate word recognition and phonology

Students with this profile need more emphasis on vocabulary and comprehension training than they do on word recognition. Their lessons need to be constructed around text at their instructional reading level (90–95 percent accuracy) and typically involve these kinds of activities:

- Establish a purpose for reading.
- Activate prior knowledge or build prerequisite knowledge of the topic or story.
- Anticipate the organization of the text (narrative or expository text structure).
- Preview key vocabulary.
- Preview the text themes, and raise questions about the text before reading.
- Visualize during reading, in response to queries.
- Ask questions or reread the text if it does not make sense.
- Paraphrase during reading, in response to queries.
- Summarize after reading.
- Connect meanings to self or world.

While it can be helpful for the teacher to model these strategies and to show students by thinking aloud how a good reader navigates a text, the most effective instruction involves close reading, facilitated by instructional dialogue, of engaging text. The pivotal skill in instruction is the teacher's questioning process, as we explored in Module 6 of LETRS. Since the questions will vary with the meanings in the text that is being read, there is no stock formula or program package that can substitute for well-planned teaching. There are many books and resources with graphic organizers, generic strategies, and activities that can be used as supplements to this kind of content-focused instruction.

Exercise 4.1 | Consider Individual Differences When Planning Instruction

- You need some classroom data for this exercise. You may use data from your own students or data from the kindergarten and first-grade classes included in Chapter 2 of this module. You should have enough data to answer these questions:

1. About how many students appear to need a comprehensive, non-specialized approach to instruction that involves all major components of instruction?

   _____

2. Are there any students who appear to have much better comprehension than they have word recognition skills?

   _____

3. Are there any students who appear to have much better word recognition skills than they have comprehension?

   _____

4. Are there any students who appear to have a very specific problem with fluency?

   _____

5. Do you have data on any students that suggest that they can read much better than they can spell and write?

   _____

Given the profile of the class (and given more resources than you probably have), what might be an ideal match between instructional approaches we have outlined and the various students in the class? To do this exercise, consider using individual data summary cards for students that you can then sort into groups with similar profiles (see example, next page). Label the groups; what do these students have in common? Then, consider whether you have (or have available) the teaching materials or resources that would suit the needs of those students.

	Group 1	Group 2	Group 3	Group 4	Group 5
Some Risk (less severe)					
At Risk (more severe)					

No matter how data-based and well thought out our choices of programs and approaches might be, we still have to determine whether the instruction is working for the student(s). It is not enough to assign students to a program, intervention group, or tutorial session and then walk away and hope for the best. Making educated guesses about students' instructional needs is only the beginning of the intervention process. The central question in an RtI framework is, "Is the help helping?" And the best way to determine that is through close monitoring of student progress as instruction is being implemented.

Progress-Monitoring Assessments

Screening, diagnostic assessment, and organization of instructional resources within an RtI framework are all aimed at accelerating students' growth. If instruction is not helping a student achieve a well-defined goal, something about the instruction may have to be changed. The decision about whether to change, what to change, and why it should be changed must be based on easily obtained information. In addition to brief tests of specific skills, the information can include observations of student response patterns, work products, and self-assessment (interview). One important indicator is the student's attitude and behavior: If students know they are learning and succeeding, their mood and motivation usually reflect enthusiasm and confidence.

Direct assessment of student progress can be accomplished with curriculum-based measurements (CBMs) (Jenkins, Hudson, & Johnson, 2007; Jenkins, Hudson, & Lee, 2007) or with diagnostic teaching protocols.

The Definition and History of Curriculum-Based Measurement (CBM)

The measures most often used to monitor progress in reading are 1-minute timed samples of oral reading fluency. ORF is both a desirable quality of reading and a measurable indicator of overall reading proficiency (see Module 5 of LETRS). ORF encompasses many underlying processes that must be executed in automatic and synchronous fashion. Until instruction is attempted, we cannot always know where the breakdowns in student learning may occur or how readily the student will respond to good teaching. Thus, homing in the best approach to teaching may require some experimentation and ongoing evaluation of student learning.

CBMs for reading fluency were developed more than 30 years ago at the University of Minnesota by Stan Deno and colleagues (Howell et al., in press; Hosp, Hosp, & Howell, 2007; Shinn, 1995). CBMs sample content that students should master by the end of the grade level that the measure represents. CBMs allow teachers to determine whether skills are being acquired at an adequate pace or rate so that students can meet the reading proficiency goal by the end of the school year. The defining characteristics of CBMs are as follows:

- They are reliable and valid (unlike many informal measures).
- The tasks are standardized and include reading aloud from equivalent passages and/or selecting missing words in maze passages.
- The stimulus materials may be drawn from instructional materials, but only if their difficulty is calibrated to match other standardized grade-level passages.
- They include specific requirements for administration, student directions, and scoring procedures. This level of standardization is required to ensure reliability and validity of the data for both individuals and groups. These standards also allow for the development of local norms.
- Many equivalent forms allow for frequent, repeated assessment without loss of reliability.

CBMs should be distinguished from skill mastery measures, which are built into many core, comprehensive reading programs and supplemental programs. Teachers use mastery measures (e.g., weekly tests, unit tests, theme tests) to assess if a student has mastered what was taught over a short time span rather than to assess student progress toward a predetermined annual goal. Mastery tests are also important for determining the pattern of student progress and should be used with students who are not yet ready to take the ORF assessment or who are working on related skills. A comparison of these two types of assessments is in *Table 4.1*.

Table 4.1   Comparison of Mastery Measures and CBMs

Mastery Measures	CBMs
Focused on specific skills taught during a lesson or unit.	Measure what should be known by the end of the academic year.
Given after a unit or sequence of lessons designed to promote mastery.	Used for monitoring progress toward that end-of-year goal.
Are informal and not standardized.	Are standardized, reliable, and valid.
Scaffolds, supports, and adjustments are allowed.	Require standard administration and scoring.

Problem-solving within an RtI framework requires the teacher (or team of teachers) to use a scientific approach. Hypotheses about the kind of instruction that is likely to work—based on the component model—are generated from data. Hypotheses are tested using specific methodologies, lesson plans and routines, content, and materials. A teaching experiment is conducted over a predetermined period of time. The effects of teaching are measured with CBMs and other observations, and the cycle begins again.

This hypothesis-testing approach is the heart of RtI. The information about subgroups of students with reading difficulties (already emphasized in LETRS) directs us to generate informed hypotheses about what we will find as we screen, diagnose, and monitor students. Those working hypotheses, for a typical classroom of primary-grade students, can be stated as follows:

- No more than 10 percent of a class should be in the range of "severe deficit" if classroom instruction (Tier 1) and small-group support (Tier 2) are effective.
- No more than 40 percent—ideally, no more than 20 percent—should be below benchmark.
- The majority will need a comprehensive approach to instruction that addresses phonology, word recognition, fluency, vocabulary, and comprehension.
- A few will have specific strengths and weaknesses that require a specific focus, as discussed in the beginning of this chapter.
- Reading, oral language, and writing should be linked throughout instruction.
- Students who are not remembering information from day to day, who are very confused or frustrated, and who are not progressing in spite of instruction probably need a comprehensive assessment for special education eligibility. Instruction should not stop while this is taking place.

Monitoring Skill Development With Mastery Tests

If the focus of intervention is the mastery of a specific skill or concept, direct measures are appropriate. Simply put, did the student learn what was taught or what will underlie future progress? Examples of such skill mastery tests are in Beck, Anderson, and Conrad (2009) and include such targets as:

- accuracy and speed of writing the alphabet (lowercase and/or uppercase);
- accuracy of phoneme segmentation, using sound boxes;
- accuracy and speed of sound-symbol associations;
- accuracy and speed of reading words with specific vowel spellings;
- accuracy and speed of irregular word ("sight" word) recognition;
- accuracy in classifying vocabulary words by semantic category;
- fluency in sentence copying; and
- fluency in generating sentences with several target words.

We recommend that these skill checks be kept short and used fairly frequently when students are ready to demonstrate mastery of important target skills. Simple charting techniques involve checking correct responses and "archiving" a skill assessment after the student has succeeded on it several times.

ORF will not be appropriate for very young students or students who function below a mid-first grade level because there will be "floor" effects: the student won't be able to do the task, so not much constructive information is gained.

How to Monitor Progress With CBMs

How progress-monitoring with ORF is conducted

Curriculum-based measures, including ORF, typically involve 1-minute timed readings or 3-minute Maze passages. Scores are simply the number of correct and incorrect responses. To improve reliability, reading fluency or other skills are sampled several times with different reading passages. For example, the *DIBELS* ORF measure includes three passages for screening and 20 equivalent passages for monitoring progress. One major improvement in *DIBELS Next* is the carefully documented equivalency of the passages.

ORF is meaningful to use for progress-monitoring once the student can read connected text and is accurate on or knows how to decode the words to be read in the passage. Administration of ORF in progress-monitoring makes the most sense when the major goal of instruction is increasing passage-reading fluency to the benchmark level. ORF, however, does not directly address specific aspects of comprehension that a teacher may want to assess, or specific decoding skills that have been studied.

Although progress-monitoring on ORF is usually done with grade-level passages, students with serious reading difficulties who are far below grade level should read from text that is one or two levels below the grade-level norm. Since they must read from unpracticed text, it should be within a difficulty level they can handle, defined as a 90 percent or better success rate.

Standardized assessment

Progress-monitoring passages, even if out-of-level, should be used in a standardized way (e.g., there are rules for scoring errors). On most CBM ORF measures, an error includes any word that is omitted, mispronounced, or substituted for another word. If words are transposed (e.g., "out of *home* and *house*" instead of "out of *house* and *home*"), they are each counted as errors. If a word is read incorrectly more than once, it counts as an error each time. Repetitions of words read correctly, errors self-corrected by the student, and mispronunciations of dialect or speech impairments are not counted as errors. A word inserted that does not appear in the text is not counted as an error in the final total, because the final score is an indication of the number of words that were read correctly in the text.

The student is asked to do his/her best reading and to be ready to tell what the story is about (*not* to "read as fast as you can"). After 1 minute, the student is asked to stop reading. The examiner then subtracts the total number of errors from the total number of words read by the student to obtain a score of "words correct per minute" (WCPM). One or two more passages of equivalent difficulty may be necessary to ensure a reliable estimate of performance because texts vary in interest and relevance to students. If three passages are used, the median (middle) scores are used to estimate the student's fluency and accuracy. If standardized passages are used in which the text has been carefully controlled for difficulty (such as those in *DIBELS Next*), a score from a single passage may be sufficiently reliable.

Charting fluency data

Students who get involved in charting their own data will be much more motivated to work at improving their scores from assessment to assessment. Charts should be designed to show small increments of gain that will become significant over time. Charts should include both fluency data (which should gradually increase) and error rates (which should stay low). If error rates are too high, the students' instruction should emphasize reteaching and accuracy before any emphasis on fluency is appropriate. Be sure to mark the goal toward which each student is working; keep the expectations reasonable, but keep them high!

Exercise 4.2 | Graphing ORF Data

- The number scores below the *Figure 4.1* graph are those of a second-grade student who was assigned to a Tier 2 intervention group that was focused on building reading fluency. The duration of the instruction was planned for ten weeks, but the intervention team decided that a change of approach was necessary after the fourth assessment (three weeks of instruction).

- Using the graph, follow these steps.

  1. Draw a goal line—the ORF standard for mid-second grade.

  2. Draw an aimline between the student's baseline ORF and where he needs to be.

  3. Mark the number of words read correctly per minute (WCPM) and the number of errors in each passage.

  4. Calculate the error rate by using this formula: $\dfrac{\text{\# of errors}}{\text{total words read}}$

  5. After you complete the graph, discuss what the pattern could mean.

Exercise 4.2 (continued)

Figure 4.1   A Sample CBM Progress Graph

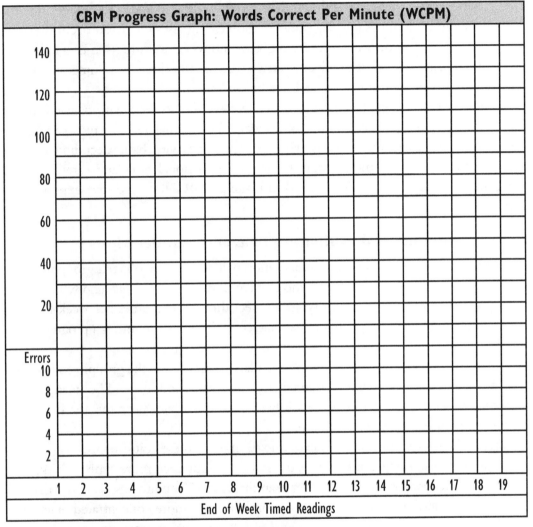

Passage:	Total Wds.	Errors	WCPM	Passage:	Total Wds.	Errors	WCPM
1._____	56	6	50	11._____			
2._____	60	7	53	12._____			
3._____	62	8	54	13._____			
4._____	60	7	53				
[change approach]				14._____			
5._____	56	3	53	15._____			
6._____	59	2	57	16._____			
7._____	63	2	61	17._____			
8._____	65	2	63	18._____			
9._____	66	3	63	19._____			
10._____	68	2	66	20._____			

How often should progress-monitoring take place?

Progress toward a learning goal should be measured as frequently as necessary to be sure of the effectiveness of the program, but not so often as to detract from valuable instructional time. Progress-monitoring is meaningful only if at least five to ten hours of instruction have occurred between the measures. If the student is mildly delayed and is receiving supportive instruction about 30 minutes per day, progress-monitoring assessment can occur every two to three weeks. If the student has a severe problem and receives instruction two hours daily, progress-monitoring can occur every one to two weeks. After three data points are obtained and graphed, a trend line toward the goal will be evident.

One must proceed cautiously, however, in the case of a student with a severe reading disability who is very frustrated and task-avoidant. Timed oral reading tests can become excruciating experiences for students who are struggling with basic decoding processes. Sometimes the instruction must simply focus on foundational skills and careful, accurate reading until sufficient fluency is achieved to make an ORF test a positive experience for the student.

Grouping students and evaluating instructional decisions

The majority of students who need intervention will be assigned to Tier 2 groupings. Those small groups should consist of students who need to *work on the same skills* and whose *learning rate is approximately equal.* The groups typically meet three to five times per week for 30–40 minutes. The lessons provide systematic, explicit, cumulative instruction in a progression that is *aligned with* and *reinforced by* the main classroom instructional program.

Before instruction begins, a plan should be in place to reexamine the groupings after 10–12 weeks. It is important to give intervention a chance to work and to avoid bouncing students from setting to setting, unless one is obviously misplaced. In that case, move the student to a different group or change the instruction.

Changing the instruction usually means one or more of these adjustments:

- *Changing the intensity.* For example, the student might need more time on-task, such as five sessions per week rather than three, or 45-minute lessons rather than 30-minute lessons, and/or a higher response rate and more concentrated practice.
- *Changing the instructional approach or methodology,* such as: (a) more emphasis on multisensory engagement (e.g., simultaneous seeing, hearing, touching, moving); (b) more focus on underlying skills; (c) smaller steps; (d) a more structured and cumulative approach; or (e) more emphasis on word meanings or oral expressive language.
- *Changing the group size or composition.*

Exercise 4.3	Planning Implementation of Progress-Monitoring

- Take a few minutes to think about and note responses to the following questions. If you are with a group that works together, combine your thoughts and reflections about how to use progress-monitoring assessments to best advantage in your setting.

1. Are progress-monitoring assessments used frequently enough? Too frequently?

   _____

   _____

2. Are you making a distinction between CBMs and mastery tests?

   _____

   _____

3. Are the PM measures administered under standardized conditions?

   _____

   _____

4. How are the data used? Does the faculty work together on instructional decisions involving grouping, program/approach selection, or intensity of instruction?

   _____

   _____

Summary

After screening, diagnostic, and observational data have been gathered, teams of teachers must decide how to allocate instructional resources. How should instruction be differentiated if all students do not need the same kind of instruction?

A research-based framework for assigning students to instructional groups is this: Most students with reading challenges need a comprehensive, multicomponent approach because they demonstrate weaknesses in most of the strands of the "reading rope." Another subgroup will fit the profile of good language comprehension with specific word-recognition problems. These problems may originate with faulty phonological processing, weak phonics skills, and/ or slow word recognition (dysfluency). Still another subtype of poor reader may read the words accurately but, because of vocabulary and language comprehension weaknesses, may demonstrate poor comprehension of text that students are able to read. Furthermore, these general subtypes vary in the severity of their problems and, thus, the intensity and nature of the intervention work that is carried out with them.

Screening and diagnostic tests provide us a basis for educated guesswork about response to instruction, but progress-monitoring assessment is an important adjunct in decision-making. Progress-monitoring should involve brief, timed readings of standardized passages and other forms of curriculum-based measurement. Progress-monitoring is carried out quite frequently with students who are experiencing the greatest difficulties learning to read and write. The purpose of progress-monitoring is to judge whether the intervention is having the desired effect—accelerated academic growth. If it is not, then the frequency and duration of instruction, group composition, and/or methodology may need to be adjusted.

This being said, some students with specific learning disabilities—especially dyslexia—take a very long time to learn to read with fluency and understanding. They need a consistent approach delivered by a skilled and informed teacher over a long period of time. Sometimes their progress is slow in the beginning, and shifting gears too soon can be detrimental. There is no substitute for the judgment and flexibility of an informed, well-prepared team of teachers who use all of these tools wisely.

Our module will conclude, in Chapter 5, with an overview of the kinds of "big picture" data that educators must keep front and center if their decisions and practices are to best serve the needs of all students.

Chapter 5

Schoolwide Implementation of Data-Based Intervention

Learner Objectives for Chapter 5

- Understand the value of class, school, and district data for coordinating and improving instruction.
- Understand benchmark linkages and what they can indicate about programming.
- Revisit Ehri's phases of word reading development in relation to designing instruction.
- Review a checklist for implementation of schoolwide assessment.

Warm-Up: Revisit True/False Questions

- We started Chapter 1 with these True/False questions. Perhaps you guessed at some answers. Are you more confident of your answers at this point? If not, what answers remain ambiguous? Do you need more information to answer the questions?

	TRUE	FALSE
1. We can predict silent passage-reading comprehension in third-graders fairly well using simple screening tests of speech-sound awareness and letter knowledge in kindergarten.		
2. Many children who seem behind in reading readiness at the kindergarten level are late bloomers; if we wait a year or two, they will grow out of their problems.		
3. A 45-minute screening in kindergarten will be more reliable than a 10–15-minute screening for predicting long-term outcomes in reading.		
4. Most reading problems emerge late, around the end of third grade, when students must shift from learning to read to reading to learn.		
5. Once we know a student's level or "tier" of reading growth, we will know what kind of instruction he/she needs.		

Schoolwide, Data-Driven Decision-Making

Even if regular classroom instruction (Tier 1) is effective, a substantial proportion of students are still likely to need either small-group (Tier 2) or intensive (Tier 3) instruction. If more than the typical proportion of students is failing to achieve reading fluency benchmarks or comprehension goals, then instructional programs and/or their implementation probably need to be changed in some way. DIBELS®, AIMSweb®, TPRI, PALS™, FAIR, and the computer-administered *Children's Progress Academic Assessment* (CPAA; see *Appendix D*) can all issue reports back to schools that answer the question, "What percent of students achieved essential reading outcomes?" These data are usually given for each class, each grade, and each school in a district.

Table 5.1 illustrates an example of classroom comparisons that are possible with data, such as these *DIBELS Next* scores for kindergarten classes in the same district.

Table 5.1   Comparison of *DIBELS Next* Results in Kindergarten Classrooms

	TYPE OF COACHING SUPPORT			
	No support or PD (3 classes)	Moderate support with PD (1 class)	High support, in-depth PD (3 classes)	End of K, *DIBELS* Goals
Average (Mean) Score				
LNF	37	41	52	40+
PSF	32	44	51	35+
NWF	16	26	35	25+
Proportion of Students in Category				
Intensive	54	28	0	>5%
Strategic	17	0	10	>20%
Benchmark	28	72	90	<80%

Exercise 5.1 | Interpret Class Reports

- Look over *Table 5.1* (previous page). If you were a teacher, coach, principal, or other adult in a school leadership role, what might you infer from these data? Keep in mind that the students in these classrooms were from the same district and were similar in background and socioeconomic characteristics.

1. Even if you do not know anything about these students, their teachers, or their classrooms, what inferences can you make?

   _____

   _____

2. What other questions might you want answers to before deciding how to move everyone toward more effective practices?

   - _____

   - _____

   - _____

   - _____

   - _____

   - _____

   - _____

3. What if the teacher(s) whose students did poorly on *DIBELS* tells you that his/her students are likely to just grow out of these delays in first grade, and that they run a fine kindergarten where students play games, enjoy activities, and become ready for academic learning? Could you explain to the teachers what these data indicate?

   _____

   _____

   _____

One safe inference from the data in *Table 5.1* is that the kind of professional development and mentoring that was available to the "high PD" group was extremely effective for teachers and their students. In fact, the teachers in those three classrooms:

- had participated in a year-long study group focused on early reading research, phonological awareness, techniques of beginning reading instruction, data gathering, data interpretation, and student grouping;
- were trained using LETRS modules;
- met every month with their literacy coach to consider data on students' growth;
- worked collaboratively as a team; and
- implemented structured, systematic programs to teach phonology, beginning phonics, and reading of pre-primer texts.

In contrast, the teachers whose students were far below benchmark expectations at the end of the year did not attend professional development on any of these topics. In addition, no identifiable curriculum or program was in use and the instructional objectives were unclear. Those teachers also did not use initial or middle-of-the-year screenings, so these end-of-year data were the only measures of student performance obtained in these classes.

How Benchmarks Are Linked

It is not uncommon for teachers to question the value of simple tests of basic skills for predicting "real reading." One kind of report that might help convince skeptics of the significance of kindergarten and early reading indicators is called a "benchmark linkage" report. This kind of report shows how groups of students are progressing on the critical indicators of future reading success. Benchmark linkage shows the relationship between the students' achievement of earlier benchmark goals and their achievement of later benchmark goals. The graph in *Figure 5.1* shows the relationship between the achievement of initial sound fluency (ISF) benchmarks in a mid-kindergarten group and the achievement of phoneme segmentation fluency (PSF) benchmarks in spring of kindergarten for the same class.

Figure 5.1 Benchmark Linkage Report
(Provided by Roland Good and Ruth Kaminski, University of Oregon, Dynamic Measurement Group.)

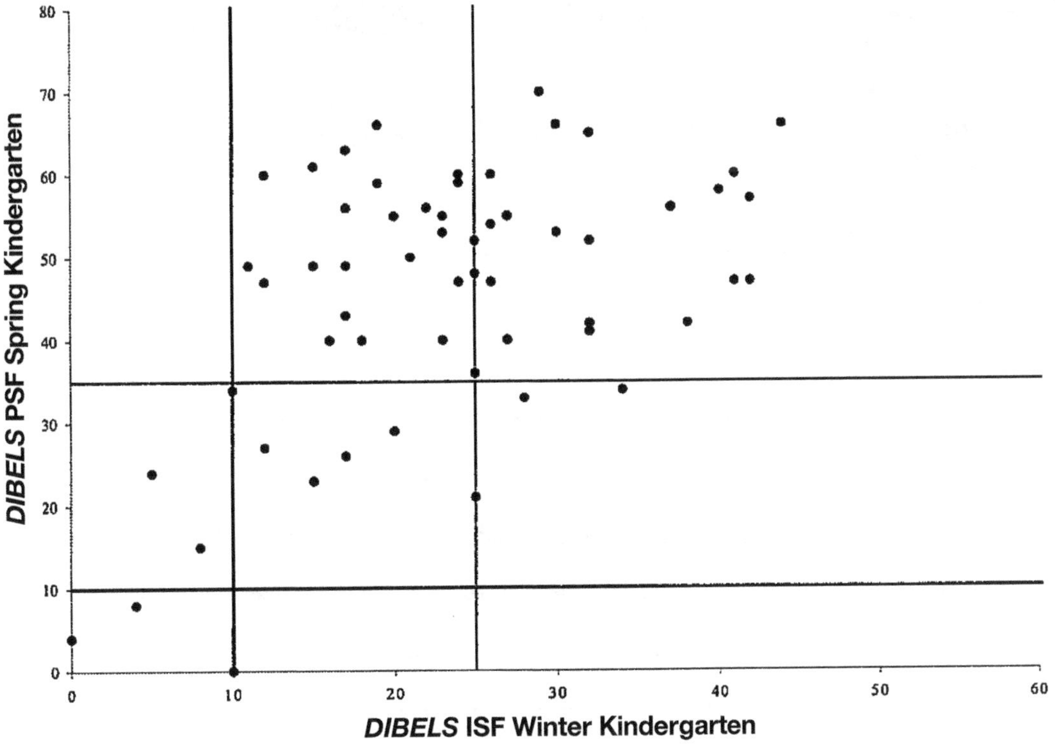

This graph shows that students who did not meet the earlier benchmark of ISF in mid-kindergarten were less likely than others to meet the spring benchmarks on PSF. Students who were on track in identifying initial sounds in mid-kindergarten were more likely than others to learn to segment all of the sounds in spoken syllables. Two students in the class remained severely deficient on both foundational skills and were candidates for intensive instruction beginning in first grade.

Benchmark linkage reports not only inform each teacher about the progress of each student but also inform administrators about the effectiveness of the school's curriculum. For example, a linkage report may show that students in a school began kindergarten with strong letter-naming skills, but because the instructional program did not include systematic teaching of individual speech sounds in words, students were no longer on course for achieving later reading goals by the end of kindergarten. Conversely, a linkage report can show that students began with a weakness on a benchmark, but because instruction was concentrated on accelerating progress, students actually gained ground in relation to the next benchmark.

In summary, linkage reports show if more than the expected number of students is having trouble with a specific foundation skill, then the curriculum or its implementation may need to be changed. Not just any change will lead to improvements; such decisions should be informed by an understanding of reading psychology, reading development, and the theoretical underpinnings that link the major components of effective reading instruction.

Exercise 5.2 | Benchmark Linkages and Instructional Decisions

- Consider the following possible results of benchmark linkage reports at the school level (i.e., combining several classrooms at each grade level). What might each of the following suggest about the strengths and weaknesses of the instructional approach in the school?

1. At the middle of kindergarten, students are strong in phoneme segmentation (PSF) but are not meeting benchmarks in nonsense-word decoding (NWF).

    _____

    _____

    _____

2. In a first-grade mid-year linkage report, students are meeting benchmark goals in phoneme segmentation (PSF) but are not meeting benchmarks in nonsense-word (or real-word) decoding (NWF).

    _____

    _____

    _____

3. At the end of first grade, linkage reports show that students are meeting benchmarks in nonsense-word (or real-word) reading (NWF) but are not meeting benchmarks in ORF.

    _____

    _____

    _____

The Developmental Phases of Early Reading

Another research-based conceptual framework that guides our thinking about what to do, with whom, in what way, and for how long, is Ehri's (Ehri & Snowling, 2004; Ehri, 2004) phase model of early word recognition. We introduced this in LETRS Module 1, but now is a good time to revisit the framework.

Ehri described her phases after conducting many meticulously designed experiments throughout her professional career in reading research. The term "stage" is not used because the phases are points on an unbroken continuum. The reason that benchmark linkages—in measures such as *DIBELS*—work the way they do is that reading subskills depend on one another. Phases in early word-reading follow one another like stepping stones. Although children go through these phases at different rates and with different degrees of effort, the phases tell us that students are likely to show one set of characteristics before "graduating" to the next. If teaching is well-matched to the student, the activities will build on what the student knows and can do.

Table 5.2 is organized around Ehri's phases of reading and spelling development (first introduced in LETRS Module 1) and can help guide decisions about what to emphasize in instruction. Do you know or have you worked with students who fit these phases?

Table 5.2   Student Characteristics and Instructional Needs, by Ehri's Phases of Word Reading and Spelling Development

Pre-Alphabetic Reading and Writing	
Student Characteristics	**Instructional Goals and Activities**
Knows some alphabet letter names and forms.	• Practice alphabet matching, naming, and ordering until alphabet letters can be named in random order and put in order.
Does not understand sound-symbol correspondence (alphabetic) principle.	• Practice writing letters until the alphabet can be written: (1) to dictation, with model available; (2) to dictation, no model available; and (3) from memory. • Lowercase for writing; uppercase and lowercase for naming.
Is beginning to match words by initial consonants.	• Build associations linking gestures, keywords, and speech sounds. Emphasize articulation.
May not understand the concept of "speech sound."	• Substitute initial sounds, ending sounds, middle sounds. Lead up to full phoneme segmentation.
May be aware of how print looks (alternating letters, spaces, etc.).	• Blend the parts of compounds, then syllables, then onset-rime units, then phonemes in one-syllable words.
May be unsure of terms such as word, sentence, letter, initial, final, left, right.	• Build vocabulary through read-alouds and theme units as well as expressive language games.
May lack knowledge of word meanings or information required to understand text.	• Stimulate verbal expression through retelling, structured conversation, and question-response routines.

(continued)

Early Alphabetic Reading and Writing	
Student Characteristics	**Instructional Goals and Activities**
Tries to sound out by associating sound with first letter and, perhaps, another letter or two.	• Blend known phoneme-grapheme correspondences into words, left to right, as groups of consonants and vowels are learned.
Wants to rely on context (e.g., pictures, topical knowledge) to guess at words.	• Match all sounds on Consonant and Vowel Charts to key words and common spellings.
Begins to read simple sentences with known words; tries to sound out whole words, but may not get through them.	• Acquire sight recognition of high-frequency words, a few per week (the goal being the first 100 in first grade).
Attends to read-alouds, asks and answers questions, and retells what reading is about.	• Browse text and predict before reading. • Differentiate question words (who, what, when, where, why, how); ask and answer questions. • Retell or summarize what was read.
Vocabulary includes the language of classroom instruction.	• Start to read decodable text with known letter-sound correspondences and high-frequency words. • Begin to spell high-frequency words accurately and to spell regular words by sound. • Learn common digraph spellings and concept of multi-letter grapheme.

Later Alphabetic Reading and Writing	
Student Characteristics	**Instructional Goals and Activities**
Can spell words phonetically, including all the speech sounds.	• Increase knowledge of rime patterns, word families, "choice" spellings for consonants, and most common spellings for all vowel sounds.
Shows knowledge of letter patterns and orthographic constraints.	• Read and spell blends and digraphs.
Is learning the most common sight words for reading and spelling.	• Read and spell words with short vowels, vowel-consonant-**e**, inflections **-ed**, **-s**, **-ing**.
Is starting to "chunk" common syllables and letter sequences (e.g., **-ing**, **-ack**) and reads by analogy.	• Learn vowel teams, vowel-**r** patterns.
Can read decodable text, although not fluently; word-by-word reading is common.	• Read decodable text with learned patterns and sight words. Increase fluency. • Reread for context if decoding does not make sense. • Partner reading, PALS routines. • Expand theme-related vocabulary. • Write and publish first storybooks.

(continued)

Consolidated Alphabetic (Orthographic) Phase	
Student Characteristics	**Instructional Goals and Activities**
Generalizes phonics skills to unknown words, then uses context as backup.	• Increase accuracy and automaticity with high-frequency words and regular words for reading.
Increased fluency in passage reading.	• Decode two-syllable and three-syllable words, using most common syllable division principles.
Recognizes more than 200 high-frequency words "by sight."	• Increase speed to 60–90 WCPM (95% correct) in independent-level reading material.
Uses context to fully identify meanings of new words.	• Expand vocabulary at the rate of 800 or more words per year through second grade, then at the rate of 2,000 words per year.
Can employ beginning comprehension strategies—browsing, anticipating, questioning, clarifying, retelling and summarizing—with teacher support.	• Deepen awareness of different genres—narrative and expository—and how they are organized.
Can compose readable compositions with capital letters, end punctuation, and most words spelled correctly or phonetically.	• Plan before writing, and stick to the plan.

So, if students:
- are lacking basic phoneme awareness (ISF), it is likely that their needs fit the profile of *pre-alphabetic* learners.
- have partial phoneme awareness (ISF) but not full phoneme awareness (PSF), they may fit the profile of *early alphabetic* learners.
- have phoneme awareness (PSF) but are just learning how print represents those sounds, they are in the *later alphabetic* phase.
- have phoneme awareness and knowledge of basic phonics but need to read whole words, syllables, and morphemes to build fluency, they are probably in the *consolidated alphabetic* phase.

With this theoretical framework, we can anticipate what students know and what they need most to learn at that point in reading development. While we address all of the critical components of instruction, we can prioritize and emphasize the next steps in a developmental continuum.

Some Key Steps in Implementation of a Schoolwide Approach to Assessment

As with any enterprise that involves the coordination of school schedules, personnel, space, and materials, a lot of planning goes into the implementation of screening, diagnostic assessment, and progress-monitoring within a "tiered" intervention system. Practical details such as the following must be thought about and addressed before data-analysis meetings can be effective. Here is a "must do" checklist for the assessment coordinator:

- Schedule data collection about two weeks after major vacations or breaks. Plan around other major events on the school calendar.
- Decide on an approach to data collection. Any of the following can work, depending on the building and the personnel available:
  - In each teacher's class, teacher and assistant set aside 30 minutes per day for four days to test each student.
  - A large team of trained people set up in a central location (e.g., the library, the cafeteria) and test all students in a day.
  - A core team of four to eight trained evaluators goes to each classroom and assists the teacher in collecting data in one day.
  - Grade-level teams coordinate their schedules so that one teacher calls out and assesses her students while the class is visiting neighboring classes for instruction.
- Provide training for all data collectors to ensure that standardized procedures are followed.
- Ensure that data collectors have stopwatches, clipboards, and testing materials.
- Ensure that data collectors have role-played and practiced testing with team observers.
- Post the data-collection schedule at least one week ahead of time.
- Ensure that each student on each class roster has an assessment booklet, and that data (if paper) will be filed alphabetically in an appropriate storage container or (if electronic) on handheld computers.
- Contract with the assessment provider to manage data collation and reporting.
- Determine who will enter the data after testing is completed.
- Have extra materials available on the day of testing.
- Remind data collectors to score tests as they give them; do not leave scoring for later.
- Organize booklets alphabetically by classroom; check against class roster.
- File student assessment booklets for future use (if paper version is used).
- Obtain reports and set up grade-level meetings to discuss and present results.
- Distribute reports appropriately and file a master copy that will not be lost.
- Return to data as instructional decision-making is carried out over the school year.
- Determine which students will be monitored with progress-monitoring tests; establish instructional goals and a schedule for checking their progress.

Summary

We have organized this module around a few critical questions that assessments should be used to answer:

- Who needs help?
- Why do they need help?
- What kind of help do they need?
- Is the help helping?
- If not, what needs to be changed?

Addressing these questions is a complex undertaking, but some fairly simple tools can be used for the purposes of decision-making. If we know what each assessment is designed to do and what it does—and does not—tell us, our instructional decisions can be better informed.

Screening assessments provide just the first sort in a reading triage system. Screening assessments do not sample any domain thoroughly enough to be diagnostic, although student response patterns may point us in the direction of understanding the nature of a student's difficulty. Diagnostic assessments should be chosen and used to follow up on the leads given to us by screenings and by observational data. They will tell us what to emphasize in instruction.

Progress-monitoring (PM) with curriculum-based assessments (CBMs) will be more frequent for students who have serious delays or difficulties. Without frequent PM, we may lose valuable time providing an intervention that is not very effective.

Finally, students with suspected learning disabilities, dyslexia, and/or other handicapping conditions are entitled to comprehensive evaluations by a multidisciplinary team whenever a referral is made by parents or school personnel. RtI systems should never be used to obscure or delay the identification of a handicapping condition, whether or not that student is responding to an intervention program.

Summary Review Exercise	**Revisit the Decision-Making Flow Charts**

- Now look back at the decision-making flow charts in Chapter 1, *Figures 1.10* and *1.11*. In addition, review other major points that have been made in this module.

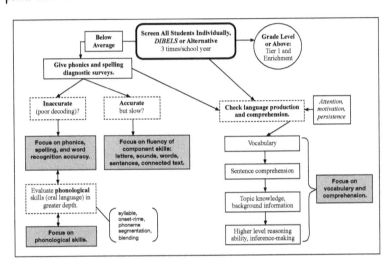

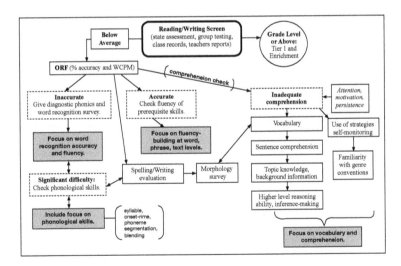

- Follow the decision-making path and identify key questions as you look at students' screening and diagnostic assessment results:

  - What **data** do you need?

  - What are you going to **ask of the data** each time you decide what kind of help a student needs?

(continued)

Summary Review Exercise (continued)

Note your questions in the space provided.

1. _____
_____

2. _____
_____

3. _____
_____

4. _____
_____

5. _____
_____

6. _____
_____

7. _____
_____

8. _____
_____

9. _____
_____

10. _____
_____

Thank you for participating in this module, and best of luck with your assessment activities!

Glossary

affix: a morpheme or meaningful part of a word attached before or after a root to modify its meaning; a category that subsumes prefixes, suffixes, and infixes

alphabetic principle: the principle that letters are used to represent individual phonemes in the spoken word; a critical foundational insight for beginning reading and spelling

alphabetic writing system: a system of symbols that represent each consonant and vowel sound in a language

Anglo-Saxon: Old English, a Germanic language spoken in Great Britain before the invasion of the Norman French in 1066

base word: a free morpheme to which affixes can be added, usually of Anglo-Saxon origin

closed syllable: a written syllable containing a single vowel letter that ends in one or more consonants. The vowel sound is short (e.g., **-at**, **-en**, **-ust**).

concept: an idea that links other facts, words, and ideas together into a coherent whole

conjunction: a word that connects a dependent clause to a dependent clause, or a word that connects two independent clauses (e.g., **and**, **but**)

consonant: an English phoneme (speech sound) that is not a vowel, and that is formed with obstruction of the flow of air with the teeth, lips, or tongue; also called a *closed sound* in some instructional programs. English has 40 or more consonants.

consonant blend: two or three adjacent consonants before or after the vowel in a syllable (e.g., **st-**, **spr-**, **-lk**, **-mp**)

consonant digraph: a letter combination that represents one speech sound that is not represented by either letter alone (e.g., **sh**, **th**, **wh**, **ph**, **ch**, **ng**)

consonant-le syllable: a written syllable found at the ends of words such as **paddle**, **single**, and **rubble**

cumulative instruction: teaching that proceeds in additive steps, building on what was previously taught

decodable text: text in which a high proportion (80–90 percent) of words comprise sound-symbol relationships that have already been taught; used for the purpose of providing practice with specific decoding skills; a bridge between learning phonics and the application of phonics in independent reading of text

decoding: the ability to translate a word from print to speech, usually by employing knowledge of sound-symbol correspondences; also, the act of deciphering a new word by sounding it out

dialects: mutually intelligible versions of the same language with systematic differences in phonology, word use, and/or grammatical rules

DIBELS®: *Dynamic Indicators of Basic Early Literacy Skills*, by Roland Good and Ruth Kaminski, University of Oregon

dictation: a classroom exercise in which the teacher repeats words, phrases, or sentences slowly while students practice writing them accurately

digraph: [see *consonant digraph*]

diphthong: a vowel produced by the tongue shifting position during articulation; a vowel that feels as if it has two parts, especially the vowels spelled **ou** and **oi**; some linguistics texts also classify all tense (long) vowels as diphthongs

direct instruction: the type of instruction in which the teacher defines and teaches a concept, guides students through its application, and arranges for extended guided practice until mastery is achieved

dyslexia: an impairment of reading accuracy and fluency attributable to an underlying phonological-processing problem, usually associated with other kinds of language-processing difficulties

frequency-controlled text: stories for beginning readers that use very common (high-frequency) words over and over, so that students can learn to read by memorizing a list of "sight" words; phonic patterns in the words are either secondary or irrelevant considerations

high-frequency word: a word that occurs very often in written English; a word that is among the 300–500 most often used words in English text

generalization: a pattern in the spelling system that generalizes to a substantial family of words

grapheme: a letter or letter combination that spells a phoneme; can be one, two, three, or four letters in English (e.g., **e**, **ei**, **igh**, **eigh**)

idea generator: the thinking process that conjures up ideas as we are writing

inflection: a type of bound morpheme; a grammatical ending that does not change the part of speech of a word but that marks its tense, number, or degree in English (e.g., **-ed**, **-s**, **-ing**, **-est**)

integrated: the state of lesson components being interwoven and flowing smoothly together

irregular word: one that does not follow common phonic patterns; one that is not a member of a word family (e.g., **were**, **was**, **laugh**, **been**)

long-term memory: the memory system that stores information beyond 24 hours

meaning processor: the neural networks that attach meanings to words that have been heard or decoded

morpheme: the smallest meaningful unit of the English language

morphology: the study of the meaningful units in the English language and how they are combined in word formation

multisyllabic: having more than one syllable in a word

narrative: text that tells about sequences of events, usually with the structure of a story, fiction or nonfiction; often contrasted with *expository text*, which reports factual information and relationships among ideas

nonsense word: a word that sounds like a real English word and can be sounded out, but that has no assigned meaning (e.g., **lemvidation**)

onset-rime: the natural division of a word syllable into two parts, the onset coming before the vowel and the rime including the vowel and what follows it (e.g., **pl-an**, **shr-ill**)

orthographic processor: the neural networks responsible for perceiving, storing, and retrieving letter sequences in words

orthography: a writing system for representing language

phoneme: a speech sound that combines with others in a language system to make words

phoneme awareness (also, *phonemic awareness*): the conscious awareness that words are made up of segments of our own speech that are represented with letters in an alphabetic orthography

phoneme-grapheme mapping: an activity for showing how letters and letter combinations correspond to individual speech sounds in a word

phonics: the study of the relationships between letters and the sounds they represent; also used as a descriptor for code-based instruction in reading (e.g., "the phonics approach" or "phonic reading")

phonological awareness: metalinguistic awareness of all levels of a speech-sound system, including word boundaries, stress patterns, syllables, onset-rime units, and phonemes; a more encompassing term than *phoneme awareness*

phonological processor: a neural network in the frontal and temporal areas of the brain, usually the left cerebral hemisphere, that is specialized for speech-sound perception and memory

phonological working memory: the "on-line" memory system that holds speech in mind long enough to extract meaning from it, or that holds onto words during writing; a function of the phonological processor

phonology: the rule system within a language by which phonemes can be sequenced and uttered to make words

pragmatics: the system of rules and conventions for using language and related gestures in a social context

predictable text: a story written for beginning readers that repeats phrase and sentence patterns so that students have an easier time predicting what the words on the page will say

prefix: a morpheme that precedes a root and that contributes to or modifies the meaning of a word; a common linguistic unit in Latin-based words (e.g., **im-**, **de-**, **non-**, **multi-**, **poly-**)

reading fluency: the speed of reading; the ability to read text with sufficient speed to support comprehension

risk indicator: a task that predicts outcomes on high-stakes reading tests

root: a bound morpheme, usually of Latin origin, that cannot stand alone but that is used to form a family of words with related meanings (e.g., **cred**, **dict**, **fract**, **geo**, **psych**)

schwa: the "empty" vowel in an unaccented syllable, such as the last syllables of **circus** and **bagel**

semantics: the study of word and phrase meanings

silent-letter spelling: a consonant grapheme with a silent letter and a letter that corresponds to the vocalized sound (e.g., **kn**, **wr**, **gn**)

sound blending: saying the individual phonemes in a word, then putting the sounds together to make a whole word

sound-symbol correspondence: same as *phoneme-grapheme correspondence*; the rules and patterns by which letters and letter combinations represent speech sounds

speed drills: one-minute timed exercises to build fluency in learned skills

stop: a type of consonant sound that is spoken with one push of breath and not continued or carried out, including /p/, /b/, /t/, /d/, /k/, /g/

structural analysis: the study of affixes, base words, and roots

suffix: a derivational morpheme added to a root or base that often changes the word's part of speech and that modifies its meaning (e.g., -**ful**, -**ize**, -**ment**, -**ness**)

syllabic consonants: the consonant sounds /m/, /n/, /l/, and /r/ that can do the job of a vowel and make an unaccented syllable at the ends of words such as **rhythm**, **mitten**, **little**, and **letter**

syllable: the unit of pronunciation that is organized around a vowel; it may or may not have consonants before or after the vowel (e.g., **cam-per**, **lit-tle**, **a-sep-tic**)

text generator: the part of the mind that puts ideas into words as we are writing

transcription: the act of putting words down in writing or by typing; the act of producing written words by hand once the mind has generated them

vowel: one of a set of 19 vowel phonemes in English, not including vowel-**r** combinations; an open phoneme that is the nucleus of every syllable; classified by tongue position and height (high-low, front-back)

word family: a group of words that share a rime [vowel plus the consonants that follow] (e.g., -**ame**, -**ick**, -**out**)

word recognition: the ability to identify the spoken word that a printed word represents; to name a word on the printed page

References

Aaron, P. G., Joshi, M., Boulware-Gooden, R., & Bentum, K. E. (2008). Diagnosis and treatment of reading disabilities based on the component model of reading: An alternative to the discrepancy model of LD. *Journal of Learning Disabilities, 41*, 67–84.

Adams, M. (1990). *Beginning to read: Thinking and learning about print.* Cambridge, MA: MIT Press.

Al Otaiba, S., Connor, C., Foorman, B., Schatschneider, C., Greulich, L., & Sidler, J. F. (2009). Identifying and intervening with beginning readers who are at-risk for dyslexia: Advances in individualized classroom instruction. *Perspectives on Language and Literacy, 35*(4), 13–19.

American Federation of Teachers. (1999). *Teaching reading is rocket science.* Washington, DC: Author.

Argüelles, M. E., Baker, S., & Moats, L. (2011). *Teaching English language learners: A supplementary LETRS module for instructional leaders.* Longmont, CO: Cambium/Sopris.

Armbuster, B., Lehr, F., & Osborn, J. (2001). *Put reading first: The research building blocks for teaching children to read, kindergarten through grade 3.* Washington, DC: National Institute for Literacy.

Aylward, G. P. (2007) Attention deficit/hyperactivity disorder, executive dysfunction, and dyslexia: The perfect storm? In E. Q. Tridas (Ed.), *From ABC to ADHD: What parents should know about dyslexia and attention problems* (pp. 103–128). Baltimore: The International Dyslexia Association.

Bear, D. R., Invernizzi, M., Templeton, S., & Johnston, F. (1996). *Words their way: Word study for phonics, vocabulary, and spelling instruction.* Englewood Cliffs, NJ: Prentice Hall.

Bear, D. R., Invernizzi, M., Templeton, S., & Johnston, F. (2000). *Words their way* (2nd ed.). Upper Saddle River, NJ: Merrill.

Beck, R., Anderson, P., & Conrad, D. (2009). *Practicing basic skills in reading: One-minute fluency builders series.* Longmont, CO: Cambium/Sopris.

Berninger, V. W., & Wolf, B. (2009). *Teaching students with dyslexia and dysgraphia: Lessons from teaching and science.* Baltimore: Paul H. Brookes.

Boscardin, C. K., Muthén, B., Francis, D. J., & Baker, E. L. (2008). Early identification of reading difficulties using heterogeneous developmental trajectories. *Journal of Educational Psychology, 100*(1), 192–208.

Brown-Chidsey, R., & Steege, M. (2006). *Response to Intervention.* New York: Guilford.

Buck, J., & Torgesen, J. (2003). The relationship between performance on a measure of oral reading fluency and performance on the Florida Comprehensive Assessment Test (Technical Report 1). Tallahassee: Florida Center for Reading Research.

Calhoon, M. B., Sandow, A., & Hunter, C. V. (2010). Reorganizing the instructional reading components: Could there be a better way to design remedial reading programs to maximize middle school students with reading disabilities' response to treatment? *Annals of Dyslexia, 60*(1), 57–85.

Catts, H., Petscher, Y., Schatschneider, C., Bridges, M. S., & Mendoza, K. (2009). Floor effects associated with universal screening and their impact on the early identification of reading disabilities. *Journal of Learning Disabilities, 42*(2), 163–176.

Colorado Department of Education. (2008). *Response to Intervention (RtI): A practitioner's guide to implementation.* Denver: Author. Retrieved October 6, 2010, from http://www.cde.state.co.us/cdegen/downloads/RtIGuide.pdf

Compton, D. L., Fuchs, D., Fuchs, L. S., & Bryant, J. D. (2006). Selecting at-risk readers in first grade for early intervention: A two-year longitudinal study of decision rules and procedures. *Journal of Educational Psychology, 98*, 394–409.

Connor, C., Morrison, F., & Underwood, P. S. (2007). A second chance in second grade: The independent and cumulative impact of first and second grade reading instruction and students' letter-word reading skill growth. *Scientific Studies of Reading, 11*(3), 199–233.

Connor, C. M., Morrison, F. J., & Katch, L. E. (2004). Beyond the reading wars: Exploring the effect of child-instruction interactions on growth in early reading. *Scientific Studies of Reading, 8*, 305–336.

Cunningham, A., & Stanovich, K. (1998). What reading does for the mind. *American Educator, 22*(1 & 2), 8–15.

Cutting, L. E., & Scarborough, H. S. (2006). Prediction of reading comprehension: Relative contributions of word recognition, language proficiency, and other cognitive skills can depend on how comprehension is measured. *Scientific Studies of Reading, 10*(3), 277–299.

Dehaene, S. (2009). *Reading in the brain: The science and evolution of a human invention.* New York: Viking.

Deno, S. L., Fuchs, L. S., Marston, D., & Shinn, J. (2001). Using curriculum-based measurement to establish growth standards for students with learning disabilities. *School Psychology Review, 30*, 507–524.

Dodson, J. (2011). *Literacy intervention toolkit: Connecting DIBELS® data to instructional activities.* Longmont, CO: Cambium/Sopris.

Ehri, L., & Snowling, M. (2004). Developmental variation in word recognition. In A. C. Stone, E. R. Silliman, B. J. Ehren, & K. Apel (Eds.), *Handbook of language and literacy: Development and disorders* (pp. 443–460). New York: Guilford.

Ehri, L. C. (2004). Teaching phonemic awareness and phonics: An explanation of the national reading panel meta-analysis. In P. McCardle & V. Chhabra (Eds.), *The voice of evidence in reading research* (pp. 153–186). Baltimore: Paul H. Brookes.

Elliott, J. (September, 2008). Response to intervention: What and why? *The School Administrator,* pp. 10–18.

Farrell, L., & Hunter, M. (2007). *Diagnostic decoding surveys.* Cabin John, MD: Really Great Reading Co.

Finn, C., Rotherham, A. J., & Hokanson, J. C. R. (Eds.) (2001). *Rethinking special education for a new century*. Washington, DC: Thomas B. Fordham Foundation and the Progressive Policy Institute.

Fletcher, J. M., Lyon, G. R., Barnes, M. A., Steubing, K. K., Francis, D. J., Olson, R., et al. (2002). Classification of learning disabilities: An evidence-based evolution. In R. Bradley, L. Danielson, & D. P. Hallahan (Eds.), *Identification of learning disabilities: Research to practice* (pp. 185–250). Mahwah, NJ: Erlbaum.

Fletcher, J. M., Lyon, G. R., Fuchs, L. S., & Barnes, M. A. (2007). *Learning disabilities: From identification to intervention*. New York: Guilford.

Francis, D. J., Shaywitz, S. E., Stuebing, K. K., Shaywitz, B. A., & Fletcher, J. M. (1996). Developmental lag versus deficit models of reading disability: A longitudinal, individual growth curves analysis. *Journal of Educational Psychology, 88*, 3–17.

Fuchs, L. (2004). The past, present, and future of curriculum-based measurement research. *School Psychology Review, 33*, 188–192.

Fuchs, L. S., Fuchs, D., Hosp, M., & Jenkins, J. R. (2001). Oral reading fluency as an indicator of reading competence: A theoretical, empirical, & historical analysis. *Scientific Studies of Reading, 5*, 239–256.

Glaser, D. (2005). *ParaReading: A training guide for tutors*. Longmont, CO: Cambium/Sopris.

Glaser, D., & Moats, L. C. (2008). LETRS® *Foundations*. Longmont, CO: Cambium/Sopris.

Good, R., & Kaminski, R. (2003). *DIBELS® technical manual: Dynamic indicators of basic early literacy skills*. Longmont, CO: Cambium/Sopris.

Good, R. H., Gruba, J., & Kaminski, R. A. (2001). Best practices in using Dynamic Indicators of Basic Early Literacy Skills (DIBELS®) in an outcomes-driven model. In A. Thomas & J. Grimes (Eds.), *Best practices in school psychology IV* (pp. 679–700). Washington, DC: National Association of School Psychologists.

Good, R. H., & Kaminski, R. A. (2010). *DIBELS® next: Dynamic indicators of basic early literacy skills* (7th ed.). Longmont, CO: Cambium/Sopris.

Good, R. H., Simmons, D. C., & Kame'enui, E. J. (2001). The importance and decision-making utility of a continuum of fluency-based indicators of foundational reading skills for third-grade high-stakes outcomes. *Scientific Studies of Reading, 5*, 257–288.

Hall, S., & Moats, L. C. (1998). *Straight talk about reading*. Chicago: Contemporary Books.

Hall, S., & Moats, L. C. (2002). *Parenting a struggling reader*. New York: Broadway Publishing.

Hasbrouck, J., & Denton, C. (2005). *The reading coach: A how-to manual for success*. Longmont, CO: Cambium/Sopris.

Hogan, T. P., Catts, H. W., & Little, T. D. (2005). The relationship between phonological awareness and reading: Implications for the assessment of phonological awareness. *Language, Speech, and Hearing Services in the Schools, 36*, 285–293.

Hooper, B., & Moats, L. C. (2011). *Primary spelling by pattern, Level 2*. Longmont, CO: Cambium/Sopris.

Hosp, M. K., Hosp, J. L, & Howell, K. W. (2007). *The ABC's of CBM: A practical guide to curriculum-based measurement*. New York: Guilford.

Howell, K. W., Hosp, M. K., & Hosp, J. L. (in press). *Curriculum-based evaluation: Teaching and decision-making* (4th ed.). Belmont, CA: Wadsworth.

Hulme, C., & Snowling, M. (2009). *Developmental disorders of language, learning, and cognition.* Oxford, England: Wiley-Blackwell.

Javernick, E., & Moats, L. C. (2006). *Primary spelling by pattern, Level 1.* Longmont, CO: Cambium/Sopris.

Jenkins, J. R., Hudson, R. F., & Johnson, E. S. (2007). Screening for at-risk readers in a response-to-intervention (RTI) framework. *School Psychology Review, 36,* 582–600.

Jenkins, J. R., Hudson, R. F., & Lee, S. H. (2007). Using CBM-Reading assessments to monitor reading progress. *Perspectives on Language and Literacy, 33*(2), 11–16.

Joshi, M. (2005). Response to intervention based on the componential model of reading. In S. Richardson & J. Gilger (Eds.), *Research-based education and intervention: What we need to know* (pp. 45–65). Baltimore: International Dyslexia Association.

Joshi, M., Treiman, R., Carreker, S., & Moats, L. C. (2008/2009). How words cast their spell: Spelling is an integral part of learning the language, not a matter of memorization. *American Educator, 32*(4), 6–16, 42–43.

Juel, C. (1988). Learning to read and write: A longitudinal study of children from first to fourth grade. *Journal of Educational Psychology, 80,* 437–447.

Katzir, T., Kim, Y., Wolf, M., O'Brien, B., Kennedy, B., Lovett, M., et al. (2006). Reading fluency: The whole is more than the parts. *Annals of Dyslexia, 56*(1), 51–82.

Keenan, J. M., Betjemann, R. S., & Olson, R. K. (2008). Reading comprehension tests vary in the skills they assess: Differential dependence on decoding and oral comprehension. *Scientific Studies of Reading, 12*(3), 281–300.

Mathes, P. G., Denton, C. A., Fletcher, J. M., Anthony, J. L., Francis, D. J., & Schatschneider, C. (2005). The effects of theoretically different instruction and student characteristics on the skills of struggling readers. *Reading Research Quarterly, 40,* 148–182.

Mehta, P. D., Foorman, B. R., Branum-Martin, L., & Taylor, W. P. (2005). Literacy as a unidimensional multilevel construct: Validation, sources of influence, and implications in a longitudinal study in grades 1 to 4. *Scientific Studies of Reading, 9*(2), 85–116.

Moats, L. C. (1995). *Spelling: Development, disability, and instruction.* Baltimore: York Press.

Moats, L. C. (2006). *Language essentials for teachers of reading and spelling (LETRS®) Module 12—Using assessment to guide instruction (grade 3–adult).* Longmont, CO: Cambium/Sopris.

Moats, L. C. (2010). *Speech to print: Language essentials for teachers* (2nd ed.). Baltimore: Paul H. Brookes.

Moats, L. C., & Dakin, K. (2008). *Basic facts about dyslexia & other reading problems.* Baltimore: International Dyslexia Association.

Moats, L. C., & Farrell, L. (2007). *Teaching reading essentials* (videos). Longmont, CO: Cambium/Sopris.

Moats, L. C., & Rosow, B. (2003). *Spellography.* Longmont, CO: Cambium/Sopris.

Moats, L. C., & Rosow, B. (2010). *The speech to print workbook* (2nd ed.). Baltimore: Paul H. Brookes.

National Reading Panel. (2000). *Report of the National Reading Panel: Teaching children to read: An evidence-based assessment of the scientific research literature on reading and its implications for reading instruction.* Washington, DC: National Institute for Child Health and Human Development.

Olson, R. K. (2004). SSSR, environment, and genes. *Scientific Studies of Reading, 8*(2), 111–124.

Paulson, L. H., & Moats, L. C. (2010). *LETRS® for early childhood educators.* Longmont, CO: Cambium/Sopris.

Pennington, B. F. (2009). *Diagnosing learning disorders: A neuropsychological framework* (2nd ed.). New York: Guilford.

Rayner, K., Foorman, B. R., Perfetti, C. A., Pesetsky, D., & Seidenberg, M. S. (2001). How psychological science informs the teaching of reading. *Psychological Science, 2,* 31–74.

Reading Excellence Act, PL 105-277, 112 Stat. 2681-337, 2681-393, 20 U.S.C. § 6661a *et seq.*

Reading First, No Child Left Behind Act of 2001, PL 107-110, 115 Stat. 1425, 20 U.S.C. §§ 6301 *et seq.*

Roehrig, A. D., Duggar, S. W., Moats, L. C., Glover, M., & Mincey, B. (2008). When teachers work to use progress monitoring data to inform literacy instruction: Identifying potential supports and challenges. *Remedial and Special Education, 29*(6), 364–382.

Rosner, J. (1975). *Helping children overcome learning difficulties.* New York: Walker Educational Book Corporation.

Scarborough, H. (2001). Connecting early language and literacy to later reading (dis)abilities: Evidence, theory, and practice. In S. B. Neuman & D. K. Dickinson (Eds.), *Handbook of early literacy research* (pp. 97–110). New York: Guilford.

Schatschneider, C., Fletcher, J. M., Francis, D. J., Carlson, C. D., & Foorman, B. R. (2004). Kindergarten prediction of reading skills: A longitudinal comparative analysis. *Journal of Educational Psychology, 96*(2), 265–282.

Seidenberg, M. S., & McClelland, J. L. (1989). A distributed, developmental model of word recognition and naming. *Psychological Review, 96,* 523–568.

Shaywitz, S., Fletcher, J. M., Holahan, J. M., Shneider, A. E., Marchione, K. E., Stuebing, K. K., et al. (1999). Persistence of dyslexia: The Connecticut longitudinal study at adolescence. *Pediatrics, 104*(6), 1351–1359.

Shinn, M. R. (1995). Best practices in curriculum-based measurement and its use in a problem-solving model. In A. Thomas & J. Grimes (Eds.), *Best practices in school psychology III* (pp. 547–567). Washington, DC: National Association of School Psychologists.

Snow, C., Burns, S., & Griffin, P. (1998). *Preventing reading difficulties in young children.* Washington, DC: National Academy of Sciences, National Research Council.

Speece, D. L. (2005). Hitting the moving target known as reading development: Some thoughts on screening children for secondary interventions. *Journal of Learning Disabilities, 38,* 487–493.

Stainthorp, R., Stuart, M., Powell, D., Quinlan, P., & Garwood, H. (2010). Visual processing deficits in children with slow RAN performance. *Scientific Studies of Reading, 14*(3), 266–292.

Stanovich, K. E. (2000). *Progress in understanding reading: Scientific foundations and new frontiers.* New York: Guilford.

Torgesen, J. K. (2004). Avoiding the devastating downward spiral: The evidence that early intervention prevents reading failure. *American Educator, 28*(3), 6–9, 12–13, 17–19, 45–47.

Torgesen, J. K., Alexander, A. W., Wagner, R. K., Rashotte, C. A., Voeller, K., Conway, T., et al. (2001). Intensive remedial instruction for children with severe reading disabilities: Immediate and long-term outcomes from two instructional approaches. *Journal of Learning Disabilities, 34,* 33–58.

Torgesen, J. K., Rashotte, C. A., Alexander, A. (2001). Principles of fluency instruction in reading: Relationships with established empirical outcomes. In M. Wolf (Ed.), *Dyslexia, fluency, and the brain* (pp. 333–355). Parkton, MD: York.

Tunmer, W. E. (2008). Recent developments in reading intervention research: Introduction to the special issue. *Reading and Writing, 21,* 299–316.

Tunmer, W. E., & Greaney, K. (2010). Defining dyslexia. *Journal of Learning Disabilities, 43*(3), 229–243.

Wolf, M. (2007). *Proust and the squid: The story and science of the reading brain.* New York: Harper.

Wolf, M., & Bowers, P. G. (1999). The double-deficit hypothesis for the developmental dyslexias. *Journal of Educational Psychology, 91,* 415–438.

Wolf, M., & Katzir-Cohen, T. (2001). Reading fluency and its intervention. *Scientific Studies of Reading, 5,* 211–238.

Web Sites for Information on RtI

- National Association of State Directors of Special Education (http://www.nasdse.org)
- RTI Action Network (http://www.rtinetwork.org)
- Association for Supervision and Curriculum Development (ASCD) (http://www.ascd.org)

Appendix A
Understanding Test Scores

(Based on material contributed by J. Ron Nelson, Ph.D.)

Key Concepts Necessary to Understand Scores

Screening, progress-monitoring, diagnostic, and outcome measures produce a variety of scores (i.e., numerical results produced by measures). Scores provide an efficient, effective, and objective way of characterizing the attribute or domain—called *constructs* in the measurement world—of interest. However, scores are tricky to understand. There are a number of concepts and issues that must be understood if scores are to be used effectively. In this section, we address some fundamental concepts necessary to understand scores.

Levels of Measurement

Understanding the measurement scale underlying a score is important to the interpretation of the numerical value(s) produced by a measure. The four levels of measurement, from lowest to highest level, include:

1. **Nominal**—Scores name an attribute or a domain.
2. **Ordinal**—Scores indicate a rank order within an attribute or a domain.
3. **Interval**—Scores indicate relative standing within a group, and also are based on an equal-interval scale.
4. **Ratio**—Scores describe relative or comparable amount of an attribute or a domain; includes an absolute zero.

Nominal measurement values simply "name" the attribute; no ordering or ranking of an attribute is provided. For example, a child's gender is a variable to which we can assign a value (e.g., 1 = female; 2 = male). A measurement value for gender simply represents a name. Because nominal values represent names, scores based on a nominal measurement scale are seldom, if at all, used to describe a child's performance or the quality of the school environment.

Ordinal measurement values "rank order," the attribute from better to worse or from worse to better; no information on the relative or comparable amount of an attribute is provided. In other words, these measurement values indicate more or less of the attribute, but not how much more or less. For example, children can be rank-ordered in terms of their height or weight (e.g., tallest to shortest; heaviest to lightest). The rank order of a specific group, such as a children in a classroom, does not tell us where any child is in relation to a national norm or a developmental norm. Because knowing the rank order of an attribute is relatively useful, scores based on an ordinal measurement scale are commonly used to describe a child's performance. Percentile ranks are a type of ordinal measurement.

Interval measurement values not only indicate rank order, but also the relative or comparable amount of an attribute. For example, on a standardized norm-referenced measure of phonological awareness, the interval or magnitude of the difference between standard score values is comparable. In this case, the interval between values is interpretable (e.g., the difference between 85 to 95 and 105 to 115 is the same). Because knowing the relative amount of an attribute is very useful, scores based on an interval measurement scale are commonly used to describe a child's performance. Such scores can also be used to compare a child's performance across measures or subtests within a measure, referred to as "intra-individual performance interpretation."

Ratio measurement values are similar to interval values in that they provide information on rank order and the relative or comparable amount of an attribute. However, ratio measurement scales have an absolute zero that is meaningful, but interval measurement scales have only a logical zero (e.g., a score of zero on an IQ test does not indicate the absence of intelligence). Weight is a score that is based on a ratio measurement scale. Because essentially all educational and psychological measures do not have an absolute zero, ratio measurement values are rarely, if at all, used in assessment.

It is important to recognize that there is a hierarchy implied in the level of measurement. At lower levels of measurement, numbers are less meaningful. At each level up the hierarchy, the current level includes all of the qualities of the one below it and adds something new. In general, it is desirable to have a higher level of measurement (e.g., interval) rather than a lower one (e.g., ordinal). Measures most frequently produce scores based on ordinal and interval measurement scales.

Types of Scores

Measures produce a range of different scores. As noted above, these scores are most often based on ordinal or interval levels of measurement. Thinking about the level of measurement or measurement scale provides a basic framework for understanding the type of information that a score provides. The different types of scores produced by measures include:

- raw scores
- criterion-referenced scores
- norm-referenced scores:
  — age and grade equivalents
  — percentile ranks
  — standard scores

Raw Scores

All measures produce a raw score. The raw score is typically the number of items answered correctly or observed, in the case of observational measures. Raw scores are typically converted because, in themselves, they are typically not meaningful. Thus, authors and publishers convert raw scores into the other scores that are described in the remainder of this section. The two major types of raw score transformations are *criterion-referenced* and *norm-referenced*. The transformations of both raw score types represent fundamentally different ways of describing the results from a measure.

Criterion-Referenced Scores

Criterion-referenced scores compare a child's performance (or other attribute) against an objective criterion or functional level of performance. The most common scores produced by criterion-referenced measures include "observed" or "not observed"; "occurred" or "not occurred"; "below basic," "basic," or "proficient," or some other variation on this theme. The scores are often expressed as percentages (e.g., the number of "observed" or "not observed" responses as a function of the total number of responses). Criterion-referenced scores are intuitive and easy to understand. Further, criterion-referenced scores are based on an ordinal measurement scale.

Norm-Referenced Scores

Norm-referenced scores compare a child's performance against a normative sample of children. Specific norm-referenced scores include the following types.

1. **Age- or grade-equivalent scores** describe the performance of a child in relation to the average performance of children in the normative group at the same age. For example, if a child receives an age-equivalent score of 3 years, 4 months (expressed as 3-4), on a measure of phonological awareness, the child performed the same as the average child at the 3rd year, 4th month, in the norm group. Grade scores are interpreted in a similar manner; for example, if a child receives a grade equivalent score of 1st grade, 2nd month (expressed as 1-2), the child's performance is the same as the average child in the 1st grade, 2nd month, in the norm group. Age- and grade-equivalent scores are based on an ordinal measurement scale.

2. **Percentile rank scores** indicate the rank of a child in comparison to 100 children of similar age or grade in the normative group. For example, if a child receives a percentile score of 55 (expressed as the 55th percentile), the child performed the same or better than 55% of the same age/grade children in the norm group. Inspection of *Figure A1* (next page) shows that the 50th percentile signifies average performance with the norm group. Percentile rank scores are based on an ordinal measurement scale.

3. **Standard scores** describe the performance of a child in relation to the average variability (standard deviation) of scores of the same age/grade children in the group. The normal distribution, or bell-shaped curve, plays a key role in interpreting standard scores from norm-referenced measures. In a normal distribution, 68% of scores of a typical group fall in the "average" range (i.e., within ±1 standard deviation of the mean). Scores between 1 and 2 standard deviations above and below the mean fall in the "above average" (an additional 14%) and "below average" (an additional 14%) range, respectively. Scores greater than 2 standard deviations above and below the mean fall in the "significantly above average" (approximately 2%) and "significantly below average"

(approximately 2%) range, respectively. The most widely used standard score scales are based on a scale where the average (mean) is 100 and the standard deviation is set at 15 points.

Stanines are another common standard score that have a mean of 5 and a standard deviation of 2. Stanines range from 1 to 9 and are an efficient way to communicate the range in which a child's score falls (e.g., "above average"). Other standard scores include the **t-score** (mean of 50 and standard deviation of 10), **z-score** (mean of 0 and standard deviation of 1), and **normal curve equivalents** (NCE; mean of 50 and standard deviation of 21.06). All standard scores are based on an interval measurement scale. Recall that interval level scores can be used to compare a child's performance across measures or subtests within a measure (referred to as *intra-individual performance interpretation*).

Figure A1   Norm-Referenced Scores on the Bell-Shaped Curve

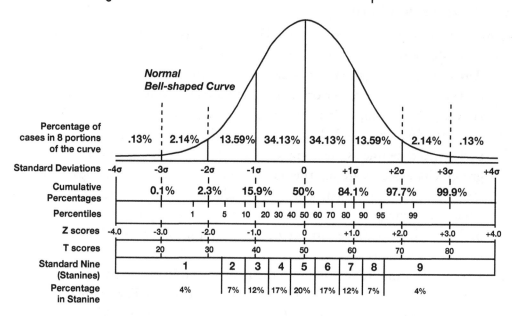

Scores Are Only Estimates

One of the most important concepts for the appropriate interpretation of scores is to understand that they are only *estimates* of the attribute or domain of interest (e.g., phonological awareness). This means that we can never know the true score or the exact magnitude of an attribute that lies within the person being assessed. The obtained or observed score comprises a true level of performance plus random error (see equation below). For example, we observe a child's performance on a measure of phonological awareness, which is reflected by the score (the left side of the equation). We are unable to observe the child's true performance and the amount of measurement error (the right side of the equation). In short, we should always keep in mind that scores produced by measures are only estimates of the unobservable "true score."

| Obtained/observed score | = | True Performance | + | Measurement error |

One of the strengths of norm-referenced measures is that the amount of measurement error is typically specified by a statistic called the *standard error of measurement* (i.e., SEM). The SEM can be used to establish 68% ($\pm$1 SEM) and 95% ($\pm$2 SEM) confidence intervals around an observed score. For example, in the case of a child who receives a standard score of 95 on a norm-referenced measure with an SEM of 4, our interpretations would be as follows:

- With 68% confidence, the child's true score falls between 91 and 99 (i.e., 95 $\pm$4).
- With 95% confidence, the child's true score falls between 87 and 103 (i.e., 95 $\pm$8).

The below 68% and 95% confidence interval interpretations demonstrate the importance of understanding that score or values produced by a measure are only estimates of an attribute. Unfortunately, many measures (e.g., observation rating scales) used with young children are not norm-referenced and do not provide an index of measurement error (i.e., SEM). In these cases, there are three possible solutions:

1. *Interpret the scores or values produced by a measure very cautiously.* The degree of caution should increase as the score deviates from average because errors of measurement increase as scores deviate from average or typical. There is little doubt that measures that have not gone through rigorous psychometric studies to establish their reliability and validity are prone to large errors of measurement.

2. *Use multiple measures of the same attribute.* The scores from the different measures can be triangulated to get a more accurate sense of the child's performance.

3. *Assess the attribute of interest multiple times.* Typically, the median score from three measurement sessions will provide a relatively accurate sense of the child's performance.

Finally, using the SEM and associated confidence intervals allows one to assess strengths and weaknesses in a child's performance across tests or subtest within a test. This is commonly referred to as an *intra-individual performance interpretation* and is restricted to scores based on an interval measurement scale. For example, the standard scores (based on a mean of 100 and standard deviation of 15) and associated 68% confidence intervals (SEM = $\pm$4) for two different children on an alphabet knowledge and phonological awareness are presented in *Table A1* (next page). In the case of Allie, inspection of the 68% confidence intervals reveals differences in her alphabet knowledge and phonological awareness (i.e., the confidence intervals do not overlap with one another). Allie shows strength in phonological awareness relative to alphabet knowledge. In the case of Jorge, inspection of the 68% confidence intervals reveals no differences in his alphabet knowledge and phonological awareness (i.e., confidence intervals overlap with one another). Jorge does not show a relative strength or weakness in alphabet knowledge and phonological awareness. Finally, although some measures provide specific guidelines for making intra-individual performance interpretations, the 68% or 95% confidence intervals can be used to establish relative strengths and weaknesses in those cases when guidelines are not provided.

Table A1 Comparison of Two Children's Test Scores

Child	Subtest	Standard Score	68% Confidence Interval
Allie	• Alphabet knowledge	80	76–84
	• Phonological awareness	92	88–96
Jorge	• Alphabet knowledge	82	78–86
	• Phonological awareness	85	81–89

Reliability

The SEM provides an indication of the technical quality of a measure and is based on and related directly to *reliability*. As the reliability of a measure increases, its SEM decreases, and vice versa. Reliability refers to the "consistency" or "repeatability" of measures or observations. A test must be reliable to be valid. A valid test measures what its authors and publishers claim the test measures. In other words, reliability is a necessary condition—but not the only condition—that must be met for a test to be valid. Although it is not possible to establish the reliability of a measure exactly, four approaches are used to estimate the reliability of a measure:

1. **Test–retest reliability** estimates the consistency of the results of the same measure administered to the same sample on two different occasions (typically, two to four weeks apart).

2. **Parallel-forms reliability** estimates the consistency of the results of two or more forms of the same measure administered to the same sample at the same time.

3. **Internal consistency reliability** estimates the consistency of results across items within the same measure administered to the same sample at the same time.

4. **Inter-rater, or inter-observer, reliability** estimates the extent to which different raters/observers give consistent estimates of an attribute on the same sample at the same time.

These four approaches to reliability provide different estimates of reliability. *Test-retest reliability* provides one of the most important estimates of the consistency of a measure over time. Most attributes (e.g., phonological awareness) change slowly over a short period of time. Radical and unpredictable changes in children's scores on a phonological awareness measure over a short period of time would raise concerns about the reliability of a measure. *Parallel-forms reliability* is important for measures in which you intend to use alternative forms. For example, you would use one form of measure in the beginning of the school year and another form at the end of the school year to measure growth in children's phonological awareness. *Internal consistency reliability* is important for measures that include multiple items that measure the same attribute (e.g., 10-item rating scale of phonological awareness). In effect, the reliability of a measure is judged by estimating how well the items that reflect the same attribute yield similar results. *Inter-rater, or inter-observer, reliability* is important in those cases in which observations are being conducted. One's confidence in the results is enhanced when two raters rate a child's phonological awareness in a similar fashion. Finally, keep in mind that each of these approaches to reliability will yield a different estimate of reliability. In general, test-retest reliability estimates are lower in value than parallel-forms, internal consistency, and inter-rater/inter-observer reliability estimates.

It is important to consider the reliability factor when using a measure. Ideally, test authors and publishers should present reliability estimates for any scale or subscale scores that are to be interpreted. For example, if a measure of phonological awareness includes rhyming, alliteration, and phonemic awareness subscales, reliability estimates should be presented for each. It is especially useful (and recommended) that authors and publishers provide information on the SEM to aid in the interpretation of scores.

The reliability coefficient is the most widely reported statistic for expressing the reliability of a measure. Reliability coefficient values range from 0 (absence of reliability) to 1.00 (perfect reliability). One way of viewing reliability coefficients is to think about them as indicators of the accuracy of a score. You begin by squaring the reliability coefficient (i.e., called the *coefficient of determination*) to provide an index of true variability or explained variance. A squared reliability coefficient of .90 s indicates that 81% of the variability of a score is true variability or explained variance and 19% consists of error variance that is unexplained. Note that small changes in reliability coefficients result in large changes in the amount of true variability (see *Table A2*). Finally, reliability coefficients for screening and progress-monitoring measures generally do not need to be as high as those of diagnostic and outcome measures. Screening results lead to the use of an intervention and/or further assessment, and progress-monitoring involves repeated measurement of the same child over time. One should expect large reliability coefficients (i.e., ≥90) in the case of diagnostic and outcome measures (Salvia, Ysseldyke, & Bolt, 2007).

Table A2   Reliability and Explained Variance

Reliability Coefficient	Coefficient of Determination	Explained Variance	Error Variance
.90	.81	81%	19%
.80	.64	64%	36%
.70	.49	49%	51%
.60	.36	36%	64%
.50	.25	25%	75%

Validity

Validity is considered to be the most important technical characteristic of a measure; all other characteristics of a measure (e.g., reliability) are subsumed under validity. Validity addresses the extent to which the measure assesses what it is designed to measure. As with reliability, it is not possible to establish the validity of a measure exactly. The five approaches used to estimate the validity of a measure are as follows:

1. **Face validity** refers to a nontechnical review of a measure to determine whether it appears valid on the surface. Face validity is estimated subjectively by simply reviewing the items on a measure to see if they appear to measure an attribute or domain.

2. **Content validity** refers to the extent to which a measure covers the attribute or domain of interest. Content validity is estimated via a formal analysis of the content of a measure by the authors or other professionals.

3. **Concurrent validity** refers to the extent to which the results of a measure are consistent with those of another valid measure of the same attribute or domain. Concurrent validity is estimated by correlating the results from a measure with another valid measure of the same attribute that is administered to the same sample at the same time (e.g., two preschool phonological awareness measures are correlated with one another).

4. **Predictive validity** refers to how well a measure predicts an important attribute or outcome in the future. Predictive validity is estimated by correlating the results from a measure with another valid measure of an important related attribute that is administered to the same sample at two different points in time (e.g., a preschool phonological awareness measure is correlated with a kindergarten readiness measure).

5. **Construct validity** refers to how well a measure assesses a theoretical construct. Construct validity is estimated through multiples studies of the inter-correlations between and among measures.

The five approaches to validity provide different estimates of validity. *Face* and *content validity* provide subjective qualitative information regarding the validity of a measure. *Concurrent validity* provides one of the most important estimates of the validity of a measure. Radical and unpredictable differences in children's scores on a phonological awareness measure from an established valid measure of phonological awareness would raise concerns about the validity of a measure. *Predictive validity* is important for measures in which you would like to predict an attribute or outcome in the future. *Construct validity* is the highest form of validity, and it takes a great deal of time and multiple studies to fully establish.

It is important to consider the validity factor when using a measure. The validity coefficient is the most widely reported statistic for expressing the validity of a measure. Similar to reliability coefficients, validity coefficient values range from 0 (absence of validity) to 1.00 (perfect validity). It is important to note that validity coefficients typically are smaller than reliability coefficients. Ideally, test authors and publishers should present validity estimates for any scale or subscale scores that are to be interpreted. Because the validity of a measure is the combined responsibility of the measure's author and publisher and the user of the measure, a great deal of caution should be used when using measures. Several factors related directly to the user of a measure (e.g., administration and scoring errors) have an adverse effect on the validity of a test.

Reference

Salvia, J., Ysseldyke, J. E., & Bolt, S. (2007). *Assessment in special and inclusive education* (10th ed.). Boston: Houghton Mifflin.

Appendix B
LETRS®[1] Phonics and Word-Reading Survey

General Directions

This survey should be individually administered. It is untimed, but it should take about 5–10 minutes to administer. Do not belabor administration of elements the student clearly does not know.

The survey is a tool for identifying which correspondences and patterns the student has learned, and which ones the student needs to be taught. When patterns are "learned," they can be read automatically, without guesswork. This survey can be used with students from the last half of kindergarten onward. The series of tasks is organized according to a progression of phonic elements and syllable types that increase in difficulty. The number of subtests given will depend on how far the student can go with at least some success. Closed syllables (with short vowels) are by far the most common in English and are assessed before long vowel syllable patterns. Open syllables and VCe are the long vowel patterns tested first because they are typically taught before other long vowel patterns. The more complex, unusual, but regular vowel, consonant, syllable, and morpheme patterns follow.

First ask the student to read the single-syllable words and nonsense syllables in each section. If a student knows at least some of the one-syllable patterns, ask the student to try the two- and three-syllable words. Discontinue if the student is having no success.

If the student makes a mistake but immediately self-corrects, count the item as correct. If the student makes an error, keep going without giving corrective feedback. Give neutral encouragement (e.g., "Nice job; you did just what I asked."). Write down the student's response on the record sheet so that types of decoding errors can be analyzed later. Encourage the student to move on (e.g., "Try the next one.") if he/she cannot respond to an item within about 3 seconds. Discontinue the survey when the word lists become too difficult for the student to read.

---

[1]*Language Essentials for Teachers of Reading and Spelling* (http://www.letrs.com).

Administration and Scoring Record

Student_____ Grade/Class_____ Date_____

Letter Naming

Say, *I'm going to show you some letters in mixed-up order. Tell me the name of each letter as you point to it. Remember, tell me the name, not the sound.*

Uppercase Letters

M	S	R	A	L	E	H
B	Q	T	G	F	J	N
Z	Y	W	C	K	D	U
X	P	V	I	O	____/26	

Lowercase Letters

o	f	e	d	j	n	k	h	l
c	i	t	w	a	r	v	g	u
s	b	x	m	p	q	y	z	_____/26

Letter-Sound Correspondences: Single Consonants and Digraphs

Say, *I'm going to show you some letters in mixed-up order. When you see the letter or letter team (digraph), say the sound that it represents. Do not say the letter names. For example, if you see "m," you would say /m/. Point to the letter as you say the sound.*

m	f	t	s	b	w
k	d	r	v	n	j
l	g	p	h	z	y
qu	th	sh	ch	wh	ng _____/24

High-Frequency Words

Say, *Here are some words for you to read. Point to them as you read them.* (Encourage the student to try the next one if he or she doesn't know a word within 3 seconds.)

see	my	have	to	she	all	some
was	of	any	where	put	for	are
they	over	what	would	these	which	your
every	once	things	does	right	because	answer
done	always	much	pull	heart	whole	although ____/35

Letter-Sound Correspondences: Short and Long Vowels

(Students recall the sound.) **Say**, *I'm going to show you some more letters. Tell me the short vowel sound each one stands for.*

i   u   a   o   e   _____/5

Now, tell me the long sound for each vowel. (If the student doesn't know how to respond, explain that the long vowel is found in the letter's name.)

i   u   a   o   e   _____/5

(Students recognize the letter.) **If the student has trouble, say**, *Now I'm going to say a vowel sound. You point to the letter that spells that sound.* (Exaggerate the vowel sound as you say the following words.)

/ĕ/, e-cho   /ă/, a-pple   /ŭ/, up   /ĭ/, i-tch   /ŏ/, o-ctopus

e   a   u   i   o   _____/5

(continued)

Closed-Syllable Words With Short Vowels and Single Consonants

Say, *I'm going to show you some real words and some made-up words. Read them as well as you can.*
(Tell the student that the second set is nonsense or made-up words.)

Real	rot	wed	bun	lap	kit	sum	_____/6
Nonsense	lom	mis	pez	gom	rad	jun	_____/6
Combined	rabbit	unfed	picnic	napkin	sudden	cotton	_____/6 _____/18

Closed Syllables With Digraphs, Doubles, and Blends

Real	twin	prep	stiff	grunt	drop	trust	
	glint	clamp	smell	flunk	shred	chick	_____/12
Nonsense	chonk	thremp	spaz	bling	steck	culf	_____/6
Combined	skimming	backdrop	upswing	complex	maddest	subject	_____/6 _____/24

Long Vowel VCe Words and Syllables

Real	dome	plate	tune	vote	chime	whale	_____/6
Nonsense	lete	pruse	wabe	pire	throme	bline	_____/6
Combined	suppose	compete	implode	unmade	insane	commune	_____/6 _____/18

Vowel-*r* Syllables

Real	fur	or	yurt	girl	chard	jerk	_____/6
Nonsense	jer	thir	zor	gurt	sarm	glers	_____/6
Combined	setter	doctor	artwork	platform	surfer	starburst	_____/6 _____/18

Vowel-Team Syllables

Real	ray	keel	mail	spout	foal	flight	_____/6
Nonsense	voy	wain	loob	cruit	plaud	wright	_____/6
Combined	sustain	turmoil	cheater	coleslaw	soupspoon	snowboard	_____/6 _____/18

Complex Consonant Patterns (Hard/soft c and g; –dge, –tch)

Real   price   guard   sledge   clutch   gem   cyst ____/6   ____/12

Nonsense   gyr   trece   woge   datch   zudge   cim ____/6

Mixed Syllables With Consonant–*le*

bugle   stable   battle   juggle   steeple

boggle   scrabble   maple   noodle   chortle ____/10

Base Words With Inflections and Common Suffixes

mittens   crushes   puffed   unknowing   evenly

dodged   poorly   frighten   breezes   guppies ____/10

Compound Words: Varied Syllable Types

daytime   blueprint   cornfield   deadbeat   earthworm   grapevine

butterfly   matchbook   playground   roadway   skylight   whiplash ____/12

Common Derivational Prefixes, Roots, and Suffixes

informative   disagreement   enjoyable   retract   prediction   express ____/6

Extension: Encoding

Use separate sheet of lined paper.

1. Write the alphabet in order. Use lowercase manuscript or cursive.

a b c d e f g h i j k l m n o p q r s t u v w x y z   ____/26

2. Write the letter or letters that represent each sound.

/sh/   /j/   /y/   /h/   /l/   /d/

/ch/   /n/   /v/   /z/   /ks/ (x)   /kw/ (qu)   ____/12

Summary Chart

Student_____Grade/Class_____ Date_____

Foundation Skill	Target for Instruction		TOTALS	
			Pre	Post
Letter Naming: Uppercase			____/26	____/26
Letter Naming: Lowercase			____/26	____/26
Letter-Sound Correspondences: Single Consonants and Digraphs			____/24	____/24
High-Frequency Words			____/35	____/35
Letter-Sound Correspondences: Short and Long Vowels			____/5	____/5
			____/5	____/5
			____/5	____/5

Decoding Skill	Real Words	Nonsense Words	Multisyllable Words	TOTALS	
				Pre	Post
Closed-Syllable Words With Short Vowels and Single Consonants	____/6	____/6	____/6	____/18	____/18
Closed Syllables With Digraphs, Doubles, and Blends	____/12	____/6	____/6	____/24	____/24
Long Vowel VCe Words and Syllables	____/6	____/6	____/6	____/18	____/18
Vowel-*r* Syllables	____/6	____/6	____/6	____/18	____/18
Vowel-Team Syllables	____/6	____/6	____/6	____/18	____/18
Complex Consonant Patterns	____/6	____/6		____/12	____/12
Mixed Syllables With Consonant–*le*	____/10			____/10	____/10
Base Words With Inflections and Suffixes	____/10			____/10	____/10
Compound Words: Varied Syllables	____/12			____/12	____/12
Derivational Prefixes, Suffixes, and Roots	____//6			____/6	____/6
Extension: Encoding				____/26	____/26
				____/12	____/12

LETRS® Phonics and Word-Reading Survey

Student Pages

Letter Naming

Uppercase Letters

M	S	R	A	L	E	H
B	Q	T	G	F	J	N
Z	Y	W	C	K	D	U
X	P	V	I	O		

Lowercase Letters

o	f	e	d	j	n	k	h	l
c	i	t	w	a	r	v	g	u
s	b	x	m	p	q	y	z	

Letter-Sound Correspondences: Single Consonants and Digraphs

m	f	t	s	b	w
k	d	r	v	n	j
l	g	p	h	z	y
qu	th	sh	ch	wh	ng

(continued)

High-Frequency Words

see	my	have	to	she	all	some
was	of	any	where	put	for	are
they	over	what	would	these	which	your
every	once	things	does	right	because	answer
done	always	much	pull	heart	whole	although

Letter-Sound Correspondences: Short and Long Vowels

i	u	a	o	e
i	u	a	o	e
e	a	u	i	o

Closed-Syllable Words With Short Vowels and Single Consonants

Real	rot	wed	bun	lap	kit	sum
Nonsense	lom	mis	pez	gom	rad	jun
Combined	rabbit	unfed	picnic	napkin	sudden	cotton

Closed Syllables With Digraphs, Doubles, and Blends

Real	twin	prep	stiff	grunt	drop	trust
	glint	clamp	smell	flunk	shred	chick
Nonsense	chonk	thremp	spaz	bling	steck	culf
Combined	skimming	backdrop	upswing	complex	maddest	subject

Long Vowel VCe Words and Syllables

Real	dome	plate	tune	vote	chime	whale
Nonsense	lete	pruse	wabe	pire	throme	bline
Combined	suppose	compete	implode	unmade	insane	commune

Vowel-r Syllables

Real	fur	or	yurt	girl	chard	jerk
Nonsense	jer	thir	zor	gurt	sarm	glers
Combined	setter	doctor	artwork	platform	surfer	starburst

Vowel-Team Syllables

Real	ray	keel	mail	spout	foal	flight
Nonsense	voy	wain	loob	cruit	plaud	wright
Combined	sustain	turmoil	cheater	coleslaw	soupspoon	snowboard

(continued)

Complex Consonant Patterns (Hard/soft *c* and *g*; *–dge*, *–tch*)

Real	price	guard	sledge	clutch	gem	cyst
Nonsense	gyr	trece	woge	datch	zudge	cim

Mixed Syllables With Consonant–*le*

bugle	stable	battle	juggle	steeple
boggle	scrabble	maple	noodle	chortle

Base Words With Inflections and Common Suffixes

mittens	crushes	puffed	unknowing	evenly
dodged	poorly	frighten	breezes	guppies

Compound Words: Varied Syllable Types

daytime	blueprint	cornfield	deadbeat	earthworm	grapevine
butterfly	matchbook	playground	roadway	skylight	whiplash

Common Derivational Prefixes, Roots, and Suffixes

informative   disagreement   enjoyable   retract   prediction   express

Extension: Encoding

Use separate sheet of lined paper.

1. Write the alphabet in order. Use lowercase manuscript or cursive.

2. Write the letter or letters that represent each sound.

Appendix C
Qualitative Inventories of Spelling Development

Administration of a qualitative inventory of spelling development is an efficient and valid way of determining a student's instructional needs. The first versions of these tools were created by Edmund Henderson and his graduate students at the University of Virginia during the 1980s and 1990s. Two levels of inventories are offered here (following). The prototypes for these inventories were shared with Dr. Moats by Dr. Francine Johnston, a coauthor of *Words Their Way* (Bear, Invernizzi, Templeton, & Johnston, 2000).

The words in these inventories contain regular phoneme-grapheme correspondences and orthographic patterns in the general sequence in which they are learned. Each "feature" or grapheme correspondence of interest is listed on the inventory score sheets. We are interested in two aspects of spelling performance as we score these inventories: *whole words correct* and *accuracy of specific grapheme correspondences and patterns*. If a feature is spelled correctly in a given word, it is circled on the score sheet. Each correct feature is tallied, and an additional point is given for a whole word that is spelled correctly.

Directions for Administering the Spelling Inventories

These two inventories are designed to assess the word knowledge that younger students bring to the tasks of reading and spelling. Use the "Primary Spelling Inventory" for grades K–2, and use the "Elementary Spelling Inventory" for grades 3 to 5, or until students show that they can spell these words.

Students are not to study these words. Studying the words on the inventory would invalidate its purpose, which is to find out what students have internalized about word structures. You may administer the same list of words three times—in the fall, winter, and spring — to measure students' progress.

The words are ordered in terms of their relative difficulty for students in grades K–5. For this reason, you need to limit testing to the words that sample features your students are likely to master during the school year. However, it is important to dictate enough words (easy to difficult) to give you a sense of the range of ability in your class. For kindergarten, you may dictate only the first five to eight words on the "Primary Spelling Inventory"; for the first grade, dictate at least 15. For second and third grades, use the entire "Primary Spelling Inventory" list. Use the entire "Elementary Spelling Inventory" for grades 4 and 5 and for any third graders who are able to spell more than 20 of the words on the "Primary Spelling Inventory" list. You should also dictate additional words for any students who are spelling most of the words correctly at the kindergarten or first-grade level.

Test procedure

Dictate the words as you would for any test. Use them in a sentence to be sure your students know the exact word. Assure your students that this is not for a grade but to help you plan better for their needs. Seat the students to minimize copying, or test the students in small groups (recommended for K and early first grade). If you exaggerate the pronunciation to clarify the identity of sounds or syllables, note that you are providing a scaffold that may not be available in natural speech. If you ask students to repeat the word before writing it, you are also providing a scaffold that should help students attend to and remember the sound sequence.

Score the test

Copy a spelling inventory form for each student, and simply check off the orthographic features for each word that is spelled according to the descriptors at the top. *Add an additional point in the "correct" column if the entire word is correct.* Note that some words are scored for some features and not others, and the number of possible points varies by words.

Assign points and analyze the results

Total the number of points under each feature and across each word. Staple the student's spelling test to the individual form. The total point score will give you a number that can be compared over time. The most useful information, however, will be the feature analysis. Look down each feature column to determine the needs of individual students. Transfer these numbers to a class composite sheet to get a sense of your group as a whole and to form groups for instruction. Highlight students who are making *two or more errors* on a particular feature. For example, a student who gets six of seven short vowels correct on the primary list knows these vowels, although some review work might be in order. A student who gets only two or three of the seven short vowels needs a lot of work on both sound identification and spelling patterns. Since the total possible number will vary depending on how many words you call out, the criteria for mastery will vary.

If X is the number of possible correct responses, then X or X–1 indicates good knowledge of that phoneme-grapheme relationship, while X–2 (or more) indicates the need for instruction. If a student does not get any points for an orthographic feature, the feature is beyond the student's instructional range, and earlier features need to be addressed first.

Primary Spelling Inventory—Individual Score Sheet

Name of Child: _____   Teacher: _____   Grade: _____   Date: _____   Total Points: _____

	Initial Consonant	Final Consonant	Digraph	Blend	Short Vowel	Long Vowel VCe	Vowel Team/ Diphthong	r-controlled Vowel	Inflections	Correct	Word Totals
1. fan	f	n			a						
2. pet	p	t			e						
3. dig	d	g			i						
4. mob	m	b			o						
5. rope	r	p				o-e					
6. wait	w	t					ai				
7. chunk			ch	nk	u						
8. sled				sl	e						
9. stick		-ck		st	i						
10. shine			sh			i-e					
11. dream				dr			ea				
12. blade				bl		a-e					
13. coach			-ch				oa				
14. fright				fr			igh				
15. snowing				sn			ow		-ing		
16. talked							-al		-ed		
17. camping				-mp					-ing		
18. thorn			th					or			
19. shouted			sh				ou				
20. spoil				sp			oi				
21. growl				gr			ow				
22. chirp			ch					ir			
23. clapped				cl					-pped		
24. tries				tr					-es		
25. hiking									-king		
Featured Totals											Total Points

Adapted with permission from Francine Johnston (1996) and Pearson Education.

Name of Child: _____   Teacher: _____   Grade: _____   Date: _____

Elementary Spelling Inventory—Individual Score Sheet

Total Points: _____

	Short vowel	Blend digraph	Long vowel	Other vowel	Complex consonant	Inflection	Syllable juncture	Unaffected syllable	Suffix	Correct	Word Totals
1. speck	e	sp			ck						
2. switch	i	sw			tch						
3. throat			oa		thr						
4. nurse				ur							
5. scrape			a-e		scr						
6. charge		ch		ar	ge						
7. phone		ph	o-e								
8. smudge	u	sm			dge						
9. point		nt		oi							
10. squirt		squ		ir							
11. drawing		dr		aw		-ing					
12. trapped		tr				-pped					
13. waving						-ving					
14. powerful				ow				-er	-ful		
15. battle							tt	-tle			
16. fever							v	-er			
17. lesson							ss	-on			
18. pennies						-ies	nn				
19. fraction									-tion		
20. sailor							l		-or		
21. distance							st		-ance		
22. confusion									-sion		
23. discovery								dis-	-ery		
24. resident								si	-dent		
25. visible									-ble		
Featured Totals											Total Points

Adapted with permission from Francine Johnston (1996) and Pearson Education.

Case Studies: Second-Grade Students' Spelling Inventories

On the next page are Primary Spelling Inventory results from three students at the beginning of second grade.

- Work in groups of three. Each group member should score one of the student's spelling tests.
- Out of the 25 words, tally the number of words correct as well as the number of correct spellings.
- Compare the three students' results and consider these questions:
  1. Which child is the strongest speller? _____

     Why do you think so? _____

  2. Which child is the weakest speller? _____

     Why do you think so? _____
- Use the feature tallies to identify the orthographic patterns or phoneme-grapheme correspondences that should be targeted in the progression of spelling instruction for:

  Amanda: _____

  Camisha: _____

  Tiara: _____

Grade: <u>Beginning Grade 2</u>   Date: <u>September 15</u>

Amanda	Camisha	Tiara	
1. fan	1. fan	1. fan	24 trise
2. pet	2. pet	2. pet	25 hicing
3. dig	3. dig	3. dig	
4. mob	4. mob	4. mob	
5. rope	5. rope	5 rope	
6. wait	6. wait	6 whate	
7. chunck	7. chuck	7 chunck	
6. sled	8. sled	8 slad	
9. stick	9. stick	9 stick	
10. shine	10. shine	10 shine	
11. drem	11. drem	11 drime	
12. blade	12. blade	12 blad	
13. codch	13. codch	13 coach	
14. friet	14. frite	14 fright	
15. snowwing	15. snowing	15 snowing	
16. talked	16. talked	16 talked	
17. camping	17. camping	17 caping	
18. thom	18. thorn	18 thorn	
19. shouted	19. shidited	19 shated	
20. spoil	20. sporl	20 sparlyol	
21. groul	21. growl	21 grale	
22. churp	22. chirp	22 chirp	
23. chapped	23. clamped	23 claped	
24. tries	24. grist		
25. hiking	25. highting		

Appendix D
Children's Progress Academic Assessment (CPAA)

What is the CPAA?

The Children's Progress Academic Assessment (CPAA) is a pre-K to grade 3 assessment and reporting program. It consists of three parts: (1) a computer-adaptive assessment that adjusts to provide the most appropriate challenge for each child; (2) immediate online reports for educators; and (3) recommended classroom activities.

The child-friendly assessment evaluates literacy and mathematics learning on the computer in 15–30 minutes, three to five times per school year (or more, when necessary).

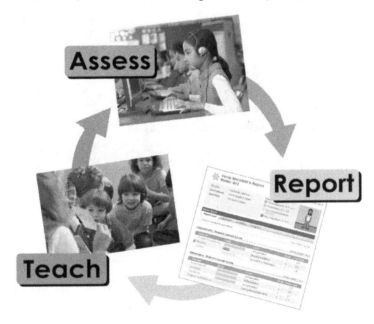

As soon as students are assessed, administrators and teachers obtain online reports detailing performance and progress by student, class, and school. These reports help teachers immediately identify where to focus differentiated instruction for the greatest learning gains and allow administrators to get a head start on monitoring program planning before the high-stakes tests begin.

The CPAA was patented in collaboration with MIT and has been funded by grants from the Department of Education, the National Science Foundation, and the National Institutes of Health. All content is aligned to state standards and is based on the rigorous criteria developed by the National Council of Teachers of Mathematics (NCTM).

Reprinted with permission.

What makes the CPAA unique?

The CPAA incorporates scaffolding (targeted hinting) within its adaptive assessment structure. Below is a diagram that outlines the structure of a small portion of the assessment (phonemic awareness, first grade). Each bubble represents an assessment item. Concepts (e.g., final sound, vowel sound) are arranged in a developmentally appropriate manner, with more difficult questions at the top of the diagram and easier questions on the bottom.

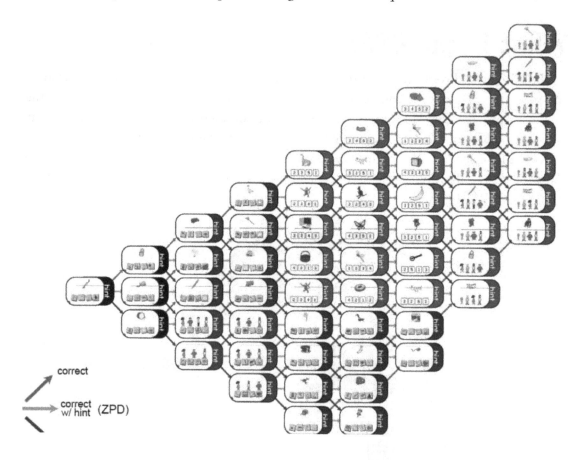

correct

correct w/ hint (ZPD)

Students start with the first item on the left. When a student answers a question *correctly*, he or she moves on to more challenging content (diagonally up the diagram). When a student answers *incorrectly*, the question is presented once again, with scaffolding (targeted hinting to mimic a teacher's careful guidance). This gives the student a second chance to answer correctly and an opportunity to learn while taking the assessment. A second incorrect response takes the student to content of lesser difficulty (diagonally down the diagram) to ensure an appropriate level of challenge. This structure is designed to reduce boredom and frustration by keeping content appropriate for every student.

Example of CPAA Scaffolding

Sample question.

Students are asked to spell a target word, **crown**. If a student spells the word incorrectly, he/she proceeds to the follow-up question below.

Sample follow-up (scaffolded) question.

If a student answers the initial question above incorrectly, he/she is asked to identify the correct spelling of the word from among three common distractors.

This adaptive approach allows the teacher to determine what a student can do independently and what a student is *almost* capable of doing (currently able to do with assistance). This, in turn, helps to pinpoint more precisely where the student's misunderstanding may be occurring.

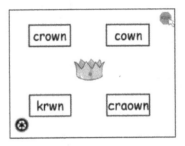

How can the CPAA be used for screening and progress monitoring?

The CPAA's adaptive structure ensures that it can be used both as an effective screener and a progress-monitoring tool. It fits within the RtI framework at Tiers 1 and 2, and can be used in conjunction with other practices to ensure that remediation can occur before special education services are warranted. The CPAA aligns with all RtI models, which call for the use of formative assessment within Tiers 1 and 2 to determine the quality of instruction and identify students in need of more intensive intervention (Burns & Ysseldyke, 2009).

Universal Screening

We suggest that teachers use the CPAA as a universal screener at the beginning of each season/trimester (three times/year). The goal of using the assessment in this manner is twofold:

- Teachers can use results to scope out the initial spread of student performance in order to proactively plan the most relevant instruction for the upcoming period.
- Teachers can identify "at-risk" students who may need additional instruction to supplement the current curriculum.

The CPAA can help determine whether a learning issue is specific to a select number of students (necessitating individualized intervention), a class (necessitating classwide intervention, such as coaching), or the school (necessitating schoolwide curriculum changes and/or professional development).

Progress-Monitoring

Once the entire student population has been screened, the CPAA can be used more frequently throughout the course of each trimester for progress-monitoring. As an adaptive assessment with immediate reporting, it can be administered every few weeks if necessary. The CPAA is flexible enough to allow teachers to choose whether progress-monitoring should be performed with *all* students or only with those who have been identified for Tier 2. The goal of using the assessment in this manner is to continue to track improvement after the initial screen and to determine whether interventions are working—and if not, to consider whether additional interventions or resources might be needed.

On the timeline below, you'll see release dates for each season's assessment, as well as suggested timeframes for screening and progress-monitoring. These timeframes are flexible and can be adjusted based on school schedules.

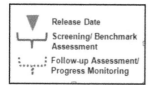
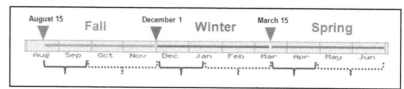

Children's progress reports make it easy for teachers to make the leap from data to instruction. The first report below, the *Class Roster*, displays a teacher's full list of students, sortable by performance in any literacy or mathematics concept. This report can be used to quickly screen performance and identify which students might need additional help.

The second report below, *Student Progress*, graphs an individual student's performance over time. Teachers can use it to monitor improvement throughout the year (or over the years), and identify whether a student is on track to meet grade-level expectations.

Class Roster

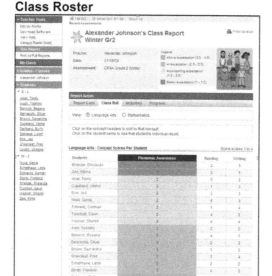

Student Progress

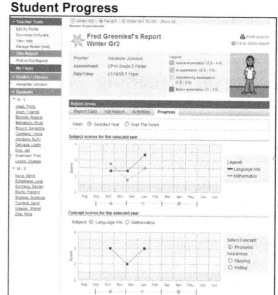

Burns, M. K., & Ysseldyke, J. E. (2009). Reported prevalence of evidence-based instructional practices in special education. *Journal of Special Education, 43*, 3–11.

Answer Key

Chapter 1
Early Intervention and RtI

Warm-Up: True or False? (p. 5)

- Are these statements true or false?

	TRUE	FALSE
1. We can predict silent passage-reading comprehension in third-graders fairly well using simple screening tests of speech-sound awareness and letter knowledge in kindergarten.		
2. Many children who seem behind in reading readiness at the kindergarten level are late bloomers; if we wait a year or two, they will grow out of their problems.		
3. A 45-minute screening in kindergarten will be more reliable than a 10–15-minute screening for predicting long-term outcomes in reading.		
4. Most reading problems emerge late, around the end of third grade, when students must shift from learning to read to reading to learn.		
5. Once we know a student's level or "tier" of reading growth, we will know what kind of instruction he/she needs.		

These questions are to get you thinking and evoke what you already know. We'll agree on some of the answers by the end of the module, but we'll keep you in suspense until then!

Chapter 2
Who Needs Help? Interpreting Screening Measures

Exercise 2.1: Compare Major Screening Instruments (p. 34)

1. Why do you think some tasks are very commonly used for screening?

    The most commonly used tasks are those that have the most reliable and valid predictive relationship with overall reading proficiency. They have been shown to be the best predictors in many studies, conducted in a variety of settings with a wide range of students.

2. Why might some tasks be used less commonly or appear in fewer screeners?

    Some tasks might be too time-consuming, less reliable as predictors, or redundant as predictors. Giving those tasks in addition to the most common screening tasks might not add very much to your overall ability to identify those students who are at risk.

3. Why do you think that some tasks (e.g., "Word Use Fluency" in *DIBELS* 6th ed.) have been tried but are no longer used?

    They might have been shown to be unreliable, difficult to score, poor measures of the skill in question, or poor at identifying students at risk.

Exercise 2.3: Interpret DIBELS Screening Data for K and First Grade (pp. 57–63)

Kindergarten Class Data, End of Year

1. What is the "risk" cut-point for letter naming fluency (LNF)? How many students are at risk? At some risk?

    At the end of the school year, students who name fewer than 40 letters in 1 minute are considered at some risk. They are considered at risk if they name 28 or fewer letters. In this class, ten students were "at risk," seven were at "some risk," and only five were "low risk" or where they should be.

2. What does letter naming predict?

   Letter naming is an overall indicator of risk level, but is not used for an instructional target by the *DIBELS* creators. *DIBELS Next* uses the GRADE (Group Reading and Diagnostic Evaluation) test as the criterion measure for end-of-year reading outcomes; letter naming predicts a student's outcome score on the GRADE. Letter naming fluency predicts reading ability because it involves naming a printed symbol automatically—a skill very close to naming a printed word.

3. How many students are at benchmark levels in PSF? Below benchmark?

   Only three students are at benchmark in PSF; 19 are below benchmark. Of those, nine are in the range of needing intensive support.

4. What does PSF measure? How is PSF related to NWF?

   Phoneme segmentation is the prerequisite skill for NWF. Segmentation of speech sounds, and identification and sequencing of those sounds, allows students to map graphemes onto the phonemes. As we identify phonemes, we create spots to park graphemes in our orthographic memories.

5. How many students are at benchmark levels in NWF? Below benchmark?

   Not one student is at benchmark in NWF in this class. Seventeen students are in the range of needing intensive support, and five need strategic support.

6. What does NWF measure? How is NWF related to real-word reading and oral-reading fluency?

   NWF measures the ability to match phonemes to graphemes accurately and quickly. This phoneme-grapheme mapping process is the stepping stone for acquiring whole-word recognition. Students must process the internal details of print and speech before consolidating the automatic recognition of larger chunks, including whole words.

7. Many of these students are off to a poor start in basic reading skills. Before you discuss intervention groups, identify the components of instruction that should be strengthened in this classroom's core (Tier 1) reading program.

   The general picture reflected in these data is that these students were not effectively instructed in the foundational skills of reading. The classroom teacher needs to adopt and implement a program that will directly teach letter names, phonemic awareness, and phoneme-grapheme mapping for basic word recognition. These students are not figuring out reading by themselves!

(continued)

8. Sort the students by their risk level on each measure. What are some possible groupings for small-group intervention?

Answers to this question will vary. The five students in the strategic range could be grouped for instruction in phoneme awareness and basic decoding, beginning with phoneme-grapheme mapping and word-building. There are so many students in the "intensive" range that a very systematic, explicit, cumulative approach might be used with two or three groups—the majority of the class. Most of these students need to be taught letter names and basic PA as they are introduced to decoding at a very beginning level.

First-Grade Class Data, End of Year

1. How many students are below benchmark in NWF-CLS? What does this result suggest about the classroom (Tier 1) instruction?

Only five students are below benchmark, and only one is in the "intensive" range. This result suggests that the teacher has been effective at teaching basic phoneme-grapheme mapping and sound blending with single-syllable words.

2. Do the NWF-CLS or NWF-WWR scores tell you which phonics skills the students need to learn and practice?

No; the NWF score tells you only whether the student can read CVC syllables (with short vowels), and even these syllables are not always found in written English.

3. Who is below benchmark in DORF-WC?

Grace, Olivia, Garrett, Nat, and Thomas are below benchmark on this critical measure.

4. Who meets benchmark on NWF-CLS but is below benchmark in DORF-WC? What other information do you need to interpret this result, and what might it mean?

Grace, Olivia, and Garrett. We need to know more about the words and patterns they are missing in text reading by giving a more comprehensive phonics survey. We also should know whether they are applying a decoding strategy to unknown words as they read or are guessing from context. We should assess whether they recognize high-frequency irregular words automatically and whether they know the meanings of the words they are trying to decode. Any of these factors could account for the discrepancies in these scores.

5. Who is relatively better at oral reading than at NWF-CLS? Should the teacher(s) do anything specific to help those students?

    Chloe, Forrest, and Art are better at DORF than they are at reading nonsense syllables on NWF-CLS. It would be important to assess their phonic decoding skills in more depth. If those skills are weak, the teacher should provide these students with extra practice and review with a systematic, sequential decoding program that moves fairly quickly through the lesson sequences outlined in Module 7 of LETRS.

6. Who looks as if he/she might be at benchmark in DORF-WC but weak in comprehension? What factors may play a role in these results?

    Chloe's retell is quite weak. The examiner commented that Chloe seemed anxious and unable to focus on the meaning of her reading. Emotional factors should be explored with Chloe, with the aim of discovering the kind of supports that will help her focus and build confidence. She may simply need more practice with retelling. In addition, her listening comprehension might be compared to her passage-reading comprehension to informally assess her verbal reasoning skills, vocabulary, and background knowledge.

7. Who should be recommended for strategic intervention (small groups, 3–5 times/week)? What is your initial thought about an instructional approach (or approaches) that might accelerate the growth of these students?

    Forrest, Olivia, Garrett, and Nat all need strategic support. It will have to be delivered in summer school or in second grade in small groups. The support should include daily practice with phoneme segmentation and blending, phoneme-grapheme mapping, word-reading practice, vocabulary, and guided oral-passage reading for comprehension.

8. Who may have a learning disability or other handicapping condition? In general terms, what kind of instruction would you recommend for this student?

    Thomas is a non-reader who may well meet the eligibility criteria for special education. He should be referred for a comprehensive evaluation while a carefully structured, multisensory program is delivered to him individually on a daily basis.

Exercise 2.4: What Can and Can't Be Learned From Screening (p. 64)

1. What can be learned from screening:

   • Relative severity of a student's problem; level of risk.

   • How many students in a group are not progressing.

   • Whether the problem might originate with weaknesses in letter knowledge, phonological awareness, basic phonics, or text reading fluency.

2. What cannot be learned from screening:

   • Which phonics skills need to be taught.

   • Orthographic memory, or the ability to remember words readily once decoded.

   • Where a breakdown in phonological processing might be occurring.

   • Whether other problems (e.g., attentional, sensory, behavioral) might be involved.

   • How much practice in text-reading a student has had.

   • A student's instructional history.

   • A student's interests and motivation to learn about certain topics.

   • The level and quality of vocabulary development.

   • A student's background knowledge and experience.

   • Verbal reasoning and inferencing abilities.

Chapter 3
What Kind of Help Is Needed?
The Subtypes of Reading Difficulty

Warm–Up: Validated Reading Subtypes (p. 67)
The three subtypes that should intersect within the diagram circles:
* Orthographic processing speed/fluency
* Phonological processing
* Oral/written language comprehension

Exercise 3.1: Review the Subtypes of Reading Difficulty (p. 71)
1. Phonological Processing subtype
   This is the largest, most common subtype. The student:
   * demonstrates weaknesses in phoneme awareness, phoneme-grapheme association, and application of phonics during word-reading;
   * guesses at words and is overly reliant on context to recognize words;
   * doesn't recall sound-symbol correspondences for either reading or spelling;
   * is a poor speller;
   * has trouble remembering "sight" words;
   * sometimes has a weak phonological working memory, causing him/her to forget sounds during decoding;
   * usually has a low accuracy rate in oral reading, and speed is often compromised because of word-recognition difficulty; and/or
   * demonstrates limited comprehension due to word-recognition inaccuracies.
2. Oral/Written Language Comprehension subtype
   The student:
   * demonstrates general weaknesses in oral-language comprehension and use, including below-average vocabulary, verbal reasoning (including inferencing), understanding of topics and ideas, and ability to construct a mental model of the text;
   * may demonstrate relatively strong decoding accuracy if the comprehension problem is specific to higher level reasoning and uses of language; and/or
   * will have trouble retelling, summarizing, extracting main ideas, detecting logical relationships in sentences and paragraphs, and knowing specific meanings of words in context.

(continued)

3. **Orthographic Processing Speed/Fluency subtype**
    This subtype is relatively unusual and benefits from fairly straightforward practice focused on fluency. The student:
    - demonstrates a specific weakness in speed of word recognition and fluency in text-reading;
    - is a slow reader even though he/she may be accurate; and/or
    - may have needed a lot of practice early in reading development to develop "sight," or instant recognition, of whole words even though he/she could sound them out.

Exercise 3.2: Interpret a Brief Diagnostic Survey of Decoding Skills (pp. 79–83)

- Look carefully at the student's responses, marked on the protocols in *Figure 3.3* on page 81, and the tally of errors. Then answer these questions:

Beginning Decoding Survey (*Figure 3.3*, page 81)

1. Of the first 20 words, is there a difference among sets? Why might the student read the first set of words accurately and make so many errors on words 6–20?

    The first set of five words comprises some of the most common words in the English language that can be memorized, whereas words 6–20 require precise decoding of closed syllables (with short vowels).

2. When the student misreads a word, does he produce a real word or a nonsense word? Does this suggest anything about the student?

    The student produces a real word. He expects printed words to represent words he knows. This may be consistent with having good oral language abilities.

3. How do you explain this student's "b" and "d" confusion, and what can be done about it with a third-grader?

    Persistent confusion suggests inadequate instruction in the beginning stages of reading and poorly established associations between sounds and symbols. The directionality of "b" and "d" can be mastered with multisensory instruction, mnemonics, and systematic practice, but is much harder to remediate in a third-grader than a younger student. Reteaching with multisensory association techniques may still be helpful.

4. Look at the words where sounds are added. What are those sounds? (What class of phonemes appears to be problematic or elusive?)

   In **rag**, **dot**, and **moth**, the student added a nasal consonant (i.e., *range*, *don't*, *month*). The presence or absence of a nasal consonant after a vowel and before another consonant is an elusive phonological feature of spoken words that we described in LETRS Module 2. Students who find these sounds to be slippery or hard to pin down often are experiencing an unremediated phonological processing weaknesses. In addition, liquids /l/ and /r/ are added or substituted in **lid** (*little*), **grass** (*glass*), and **shop** (*sharp*), and final inflection /s/ is added randomly to several words.

5. Look at the words where sounds are omitted. Where are those sounds? What are those sounds? Do these errors indicate a phonological processing problem?

   Sounds are omitted in two words with consonant blends: **step** (*ship*) and **brag** (*bags*).

6. How do you describe the student's substitution of *point* for **pond**? In what way does this suggest a phonological processing problem?

   Final /t/ is the voiceless equivalent of voiced /d/. The voicing feature is not being processed accurately.

7. How do you describe the student's substitution of *thin* for **thid**? In what way does this suggest a phonological processing problem?

   Both /n/ and /d/ are articulated with the tongue behind the teeth. The student is not distinguishing the nasal from the non-nasal consonant in the fast process of grapheme-phoneme mapping.

8. Does the student make more errors on initial consonant sounds or final consonant sounds? Why might those errors be more common?

   The student makes more errors on final consonants. Final consonants are more elusive in speech and, therefore, more difficult to map to print.

(continued)

Advanced Decoding Survey (refer to Consonant and Vowel Charts on page 82 and *Figure 3.4* on page 83)

9. What speech sounds are typically added or omitted when errors are made?

    Nasal and liquid errors are made in the decoding of lutch (*lunch*), strob (*stob*), soam (*sloam*), and several of the multisyllable nonsense words.

10. This student is a third-grader but has not mastered or internalized skills often taught in first grade. Do you think that phonics instruction to address those weak underlying skills should be a priority or that it is too late to do anything about the problem?

    It is never too late to do something about this kind of dyslexia (a phonologically based disorder of written language processing). Instruction, however, must include direct teaching of speech sounds, phoneme-grapheme correspondence, syllabication, morphology, and syntax. All components must be addressed, including vocabulary, fluency, and comprehension, although the student is far stronger in higher level language skills than basic reading, spelling, and writing skills.

Exercise 3.3: Spelling Inventory Analysis and Comparison With Decoding Survey (p. 87)

- Looking at the Primary Spelling Inventory score sheet in *Figure 3.5*, note answers to these questions:

1. What elements does the student spell accurately?

    The student is strong on initial and final single consonants, consonant blends, short vowels, and the spelling of inflection -ing.

2. What features or correspondences require some review?

    The student needs review of the final -ck rule and digraph spellings.

3. What correspondence patterns must be taught as new or unknown concepts?

    The student is very weak on long vowel and vowel team spellings.

- Looking back at the beginning decoding survey results (*Figure 3.3*, page 81), formulate answers to these questions:

1. Is there a difference between the student's ability to read versus spell words with short vowels?

    He is much more accurate in spelling than reading.

2. Is there a difference between the student's ability to read versus spell words with consonant blends?

    He is much more accurate in spelling than reading these constructions.

3. At what point in the scope and sequence of code instruction do the skills of word-reading and spelling seem to converge for this student?

    Right at the beginning—the decoding of short vowels and consonant sequences in basic closed-syllable words.

4. What could account for the differences between encoding (spelling) and decoding accuracy?

    The student's instructional history indicated that he had been taught to use contextual guessing strategies to read. He has never developed the habit of looking closely at the printed word, sounding out the word using known grapheme-phoneme correspondences, and then using context as a backup. The impact of this mistaken approach is clearly evident in this student, whose untimed encoding is more accurate. Nevertheless, he has mastered only the most basic first-grade–level spelling skills.

5. If your hypothesis is correct, how would that information influence your approach to instruction?

    Remediation for this kind of dyslexia is possible, but it requires several hours daily of systematic, explicit, multisensory, cumulative instruction in basic language skills. One rule to reinforce would be, "No guessing!" And the emphasis would be on accuracy for many weeks before fluency drills would become a routine part of the lesson structure. Cumulative development of writing skills should receive as much attention as reading, using a combination of handwritten work at the sentence and paragraph level, and word-processing aids on the computer. Further, because this student's oral-language abilities are far superior to his reading ability, he would need compensatory instruction with text-translation technology to manage the academic content in science, history, and literature assignments.

Exercise 3.4: Explain Spelling Errors (p. 90)

1. Spelling a compound word phonetically, without regard to the free morphemes that compose it: **sumthing**

2. Showing the "slide" in the long vowel /ī/: **whie**

3. Omitting a liquid consonant in a beginning blend: **thowing, fash, pat, teer, fight**

4. Misspelling a common Latin root: **progect**

5. Substituting one fricative consonant phoneme for another: **baf, flase, discofr**

6. Not knowing the position-based spelling pattern for an affricate after a short vowel: **pich**

7. Substituting a front short vowel for another that is adjacent on the vowel articulation chart: **flase, fash, fras**

8. Misspelling a common Latin prefix: **ecksperiens**

9. Confusing a possessive and a contraction: **its**

10. A homophone error that could be corrected if the base word's adjective suffix and meaning were recognized in the word's structure: **finely/finally**; **bridle/bridal**

Exercise 3.5: Reconcile Reading, Spelling, and Writing Results (p. 95)

1. Are there high-frequency words misspelled in the writing sample that the student could read accurately in the passage? What might account for this discrepancy?

   The student reads **was** but spells *wus*. He may have been encouraged to invent the spellings of high-frequency words and developed a habit for this misspelling. Evidently, he can see the word **was** over and over without noticing and remembering the internal details of the print sequence. Other high-frequency words he never developed spelling memories for are **would**, **only**, **by**, **made**, **out**, and **of**.

2. In spite of this student's ability to invent phonetic spellings for words, there is evidence in the diagnostic tasks of a lingering weakness in phonological processing. What can you point to that indicates a weakness in phonological processing?

   The liquid /l/ and syllable sequence in **Florida** (*fordy*) are not represented. The unaccented syllable and medial /t/ in **helicopter** (*hellcoper*) are omitted. The liquid /l/ in **circle** is omitted. Otherwise, the student is trying to spell phonetically.

3. Using the diagnostic evidence obtained so far, what skills and concepts would this student's lessons need to address?

This student still needs intensive remediation. Approximately two hours per day of systematic, explicit, multisensory, cumulative instruction in basic language skills—including some tutorial or very small-group work—would be needed to make any fundamental improvement in this student's reading fluency, spelling, or writing. There must be consistency across the school day, with accuracy emphasized before fluency or guesswork. All levels of language must be included in the lesson framework. This student will need technology aids for both reading and writing, but it is not too late to remediate the underlying problems that are holding him back.

Chapter 5
Schoolwide Implementation of Data-Based Intervention

Warm-Up: Revisit True/False Questions (p. 121)

	TRUE	FALSE
1. We can predict silent passage-reading comprehension in third-graders fairly well using simple screening tests of speech-sound awareness and letter knowledge in kindergarten.	X	
2. Many children who seem behind in reading readiness at the kindergarten level are late bloomers; if we wait a year or two, they will grow out of their problems.		X
3. A 45-minute screening in kindergarten will be more reliable than a 10–15-minute screening for predicting long-term outcomes in reading.		X
4. Most reading problems emerge late, around the end of third grade, when students must shift from learning to read to reading to learn.		X
5. Once we know a student's level or "tier" of reading growth, we will know what kind of instruction he/she needs.		X

Exercise 5.1: Interpret Class Reports (p. 123)

1. Even if you do not know anything about these students, their teachers, or their classrooms, what inferences can you make?

    The three classrooms with no support or professional development are doing poorly in preparing their students for first-grade reading success; more than two-thirds of the students are at risk for reading failure. The three classrooms with a high degree of support and professional development have implemented instruction that brought all but 10 percent of the students to benchmark levels. The 10 percent who are in the "strategic" range are experiencing mild difficulties, not severe problems.

2. What other questions might you want answers to before deciding how to move everyone toward more effective practices?

    - **Are there any material differences between the higher-performing and lower-performing classes?**

    - **Are the classrooms all properly equipped?**

    - **Is there a full-day kindergarten class(es)?**

    - **Do the teachers in the lower-performing classes know about the science of early reading development and the prevention of reading failure?**

    - **Is there a barrier caused by training, belief systems, or the context of the school environment or resources?**

    - **Do both the teachers and the principal share the belief that these results are unsatisfactory? Are they open to learning a more effective approach?**

    - **What did the coach or support team do to help the more successful teachers?**

3. What if the teacher(s) whose students did poorly on *DIBELS* tells you that his/her students are likely to just grow out of these delays in first grade, and that they run a fine kindergarten where students play games, enjoy activities, and become ready for academic learning? Could you explain to the teachers what these data indicate?

    With an emphasis on predictive statistics and information on how students learn to read, we could explain why students should be at benchmark levels by the end of kindergarten. There is no evidence that students are likely to grow out of these delays. There is strong evidence, summarized in the Report of the National Reading Panel and elsewhere, that first-grade readiness has long-term payoffs. Kindergartens that include instruction in letter knowledge, phoneme awareness, and the alphabetic principle are much more likely to enable beginning reading success than programs without those components.

Exercise 5.2: Benchmark Linkages and Instructional Decisions (p. 126)

1. At the middle of kindergarten, students are strong in phoneme segmentation (PSF) but are not meeting benchmarks in nonsense-word decoding (NWF).

   Instruction may not include the application of PA to the acquisition of phoneme-grapheme correspondence and sound-blending skills. PA does not transfer by itself!

2. In a first-grade mid-year linkage report, students are meeting benchmark goals in phoneme segmentation (PSF) but are not meeting benchmarks in nonsense-word (or real-word) decoding (NWF).

   The instructional program is probably not strong enough in teaching left-to-right sound-blending of written words and application of that skill to building whole-word recognition. Whole-word recognition (or reading "by sight") develops with word- and phrase-reading practice, after students learn to map graphemes to phonemes.

3. At the end of first grade, linkage reports show that students are meeting benchmarks in nonsense-word (or real-word) reading (NWF) but are not meeting benchmarks in ORF.

   Students may not be getting enough practice with reading itself. At first grade, students should be reading manageable text at least 20 minutes per day.

Summary Review Exercise: Revisit the Decision-Making Flow Charts (p. 133)

Possible questions:

1. How severe or serious is the problem relative to local or national norms?
2. Is the problem with specific "strands of the reading rope" or with most/all of them?
3. Is the student inaccurate and/or slow in word recognition and/or unable to comprehend?
4. Where is the student in the progression of phonological and orthographic skills depicted in Ehri's framework of reading/spelling development or Tolman's "hourglass" figure?
5. What exactly are the symbols, sounds, words, text-reading skills, etc., that the student needs to learn next?
6. Do I have a scope and sequence that will guide my decisions?
7. Does the reading/spelling problem overlap with other problems that may need further assessment or intervention?
8. *Who* is going to provide the instruction, *when* will the instruction be provided, for *how long* will the instruction be provided, and with *what* teaching tool(s) will the instruction be provided?
9. What is my plan for monitoring student progress?
10. What are the options if a student is not responding well to instruction?

Index

Note: Page numbers in *italics* refer to the Answer Key.

I

L